The Humans Are Winning

A Guide for Healing Trauma and Restoring Hope

Tawnya Williams

Copyright © 2022 by Tawnya Williams. All rights reserved. No part of this publication may be reproduced or distributed in any form, physical or electronic, or my any means or stored in a data base retrieval system without the prior written permission of the author.

Contact information: tawnya@ennspire.com or ennspire.com

ISBN: 9798356653766

First Edition

Cover concept: Mark Williams
Cover artwork: Tawnya Williams
Cover design: MacKenzie Freeman

Chapter illustrations courtesy of mondaymandala.com

Acknowledgements

Although there are many people who have been a part of my healing journey, there are four I'd like to thank for their influence in my life. Without these four people I would not be in this place of healing, growing, and sharing my journey. I'm deeply grateful for them each day I draw breath.

I'll start with Jamie. She's an intuitive with whom I have worked for several years now. Her guidance has helped me piece together the people, places, and modalities that have shaped this journey. She aided me in getting back in touch with the sensations associated with my intuition, which helped me gain confidence in the choices I was making to change the direction of my life. Jamie is kind, yet honest. She delivered messages that spared my feelings but did not spare the words. I've felt heard and seen every time I've worked with Jamie. And since my deepest wound is related to feeling invisible, I've experienced deep healing just being in Jamie's presence. Each time we've worked together I've been able to expand further, heal more deeply, and better understand myself. I've found deep and powerful meaning in my life through my work with Jamie. I'm profoundly grateful for her expertise and care.

Jane is a Shamanic healer and teacher. I was introduced to Jane through an astrologer, who had previously worked with Jane. Through an astrology reading, the idea of a "soul retrieval" was introduced to me because of the abuse I had endured as a child. As I understand it, this is when pieces of your soul disconnect during extreme events or trauma. The event is so traumatic that a piece of your soul must take part of that pain and hold it so the human can survive the experience and the aftermath. In a soul retrieval, that piece of you is healed and welcomed back into the present, allowing you to *feel more whole*. This is an intense and deeply moving experience.

While working with Jane, she also has facilitated several "ancestral healings" for me and my family line. Again, as I understand it, ancestral healings allow me to heal from a traumatic event. Through this act of healing, several lines of my ancestry were healed, backward in time and in future generations. Given the chaotic nature of my childhood, having the opportunity to heal myself and my lineage feels like the one thing I can do to help heal any future generations. It helps clear up past karma accumulated through my family lines. All of this work helps heal me and contributes to healing the collective. I didn't have the gift of a child, so this is how I do my bit.

All of this to illustrate how much Jane has changed my life on a very deep and profound level. Being in Jane's presence—always remote by the way—I can tactilely feel her build the *container* as she speaks. The experience of being in a *container* with Jane is... existential. I'm in awe of her ability to travel through space and time to gather lost hurting pieces of me and gently guide them home to my heart. The way Jane holds space and moves through her work is like being transported to another dimension, without ever leaving the zafu (a meditation cushion). I cannot say enough and yet mere words cannot communicate the gratitude and respect I hold for Jane.

Isaac is the first man I've felt safe with in my entire life, apart from my current husband. Isaac is a teacher, group facilitator, and healer. I've worked one-on-one with Isaac, in partnership with my husband and in small groups. He's actually the first group facilitator who made me feel safe in a group setting. It was during a medicine ceremony with Isaac when I experienced my divinity moment. During that same journey I also had my greatest personal breakthrough in terms of taking my power back from the forces of abuse. Isaac worked with me for hours as I allowed myself to experience this deep darkness and fear, while guiding me to find my own strength through this process to create my own liberation.

Each medicine journey has changed me in some way, this specific medicine journey changed everything I believe about the universe, we as humans in that universe, and the deep connectedness of it all. This was my Divinity moment. One can never be the same after an experience of this nature. I'm grateful to Isaac for each journey I have had the honor to experience with him, but more than that, I'm deeply grateful to Isaac for helping heal my fear of men. Doing any kind of healing work we have to be vulnerable or it won't produce results. Medicine work takes being vulnerable to a new level, at least for me. Feeling safe, open, seen, heard, and vulnerable with a man has been a paradigm changing experience. I'm deeply grateful to Isaac for all he has helped me accomplish and for his service to the collective.

Last but by no means least I extend deep gratitude to Doug, the man who helped shape my words and thoughts so I could tell my story. This story was never meant to see the light of day, so it was part of *my dark night of the soul* to get to this point. Doug made me feel comfortable from our very first conversation. He understood from the start that my intention in publishing this book is for my experiences to act as a blueprint or backdrop against my readers' own unique experiences as they chart their own self-discovery course. This is so they may use my journey as a guide or inspiration for how to begin or continue their own healing journeys. I'm deeply grateful to Doug for helping me get this work out into the collective where it can finally be of service.

Dedication

This book is dedicated to my husband, Mark.

Mark is the first human to look me in the eye and tell me he loves me. And I believe him every single time.

Mark and I are having the most remarkable life together! He has opened my world in ways that still astonish me. The love of one great man in my life has turned a past marked by abuse, betrayal, and poverty to a life with a solid foundation with which I'm able to finally feel what home means. I now believe there's someone on the planet who cares that I exist. He has been my rock these past few years as I've writhed around in darkness and pain to heal myself. He has never told me to "get over" my past. He has held my hand through every situation, never trying to fix it, even though he desperately wanted to. Instead, he cheered me on and kept catching me each time I'd fall. There have been times when I've pushed him away through my triggers and abandonment issues, and yet he is still here. I've never felt confidence in another person the way I feel with my husband. He's my dream come true, my modern-day prince charming. He has saved me in every way another person can and yet he treats me as a partner. After all these years together I still find myself staring at him, reminding myself he's real.

I'll never be able to adequately express the depths of my love for Mark, but I'll delight in a lifetime of trying.

Mark, thank you for seeing me. Thank you for loving me. Thank you for opening your heart to me and treating my heart with such tenderness. You opened the world for me and have helped me replace my darkness and fear with beauty and curiosity. I love you more with each passing day that I have the honor of being your wife. I'm deeply grateful for this adventure we're on together. I look forward to holding your hand and walking beside you for as long as time allows.

As in the song, "All I Know So Far," by Pink, "I will be with you 'til the world blows up!"

Disclaimer

This book details the author's personal experiences with and opinions about coping with recovering from trauma. The author is not a healthcare or mental health provider.

The author and publisher are providing this book and its contents on an "as is" basis and make no representations or warranties of any kind with respect to this book or its contents. The author and publisher disclaim all such representations and warranties, including for example treatments, methods, medications, or other counseling services. In addition, the author and publisher do not represent or warrant that the information accessible via this book is accurate, complete, or current.

The statements made about products and services have not been evaluated by the U.S. Food and Drug Administration or governing professional entities. They are not intended to diagnose, treat, cure, or prevent any condition or disease. Please consult with your own physician or healthcare specialist regarding the suggestions and recommendations made in this book.

Except as specifically stated in this book, neither the author or publisher, nor any authors, contributors, or other representatives will be liable for damages arising out of or in connection with the use of this book. This is a comprehensive limitation of liability that applies to all damages of any kind, including (without limitation) compensatory; direct, indirect or consequential damages; loss of data, income or profit; physical or mental health, loss of or damage to property and claims of third parties.

You understand that this book is not intended as a substitute for consultation with a licensed mental or physical healthcare practitioner, such as your physician. Before you begin any healthcare program, or change your lifestyle in any way, you will consult your physician or another licensed healthcare practitioner.

This book provides content related to physical and/or mental health issues. As such, use of this book implies your acceptance of this disclaimer.

Introduction

Who am I? I'm a healer—of myself and others. I've been a seeker all my life. Sadly, it was the dark and violent nature of my family that initially sparked what would become a lifelong curiosity. I remember asking myself at an early age, "Who are these people? Shouldn't I be somewhere else?"

I nearly lost my life the first time I shared my story. This time I'm sharing it for those who feel like they don't belong, to anyone or anything. I felt that way for the first half of my life, but I'm here to show you that you don't need to continue feeling lost and alone.

I'm happier now than I've ever been. I've found deep, true, and lasting love with my husband. I've found compassion for the echoes of my past that come up now and again. I've walked back through the hardest and most painful parts of my life to find peace and equilibrium in my present. I've found forgiveness for myself and my family for all the horrors we experienced together. Most importantly, I've found love and respect for myself.

My life experiences and learnings have taught me that the unresolved pain from our past is determining the level of happiness we are able to experience in every aspect of our lives today. It doesn't matter how old you are, where you live, or what you're wanting to change in your life. You must go back to where the wounds were created to heal them. Resolving these old patterns creates space and opportunity for you to make different life choices and therefore have different outcomes. I have learned through my journey that none of us is ever truly broken, no matter how hopeless a situation may feel. We are all suffering to one degree or another and we want our suffering to end.

To further complicate matters throughout my professional career, I consistently observed the following troubling pattern: If people are having problems at work, they're taking those problems home. If people are having issues at home, they're bringing them to work. No one can live a half-life, between work and home. I'm no exception.

Always the *rebel*, I decided to try anything and everything to heal the wounds of my past so I could thrive in my present. In my experience, traditional talk therapy never seemed to go far enough to help individuals make real permanent change in their lives. That's why I decided to cast the net far and wide for any and all tools, teachers, modalities, etc. that could help me heal my own suffering.

Thus far my healing journey has included: Talk therapy, breath work, Satori breathing, acupuncture, medicine work, energy work, body work, shamanic journeys, ancestral healings, soul-retrievals, shadow work, books, videos, retreats, and coaching engagements. Also, I've worked with psychics, mediums, and clairvoyant astrologers.

My motto: Leave no stone unturned.

I'm now at the ten-year mark on this journey having experienced so many tools and people to heal myself. One thing I can say for certain is that you cannot heal the present without clearing the past. The experiences of our past create belief and behavior patterns that, left unchecked, will last a lifetime. My seven-year-old persona managed all of my relationships based on my early traumatic experiences until my mid-forties. That was when I was finally able to heal a deep wound I had around love, trust, family, and safety.

I've found getting started truly is the hardest part. But, once you take that first step, you'll find there are thousands of helpful books, teachers, videos, and other resources out there. Please don't let the vast number of choices intimidate you. Instead, choose to celebrate the reality that there are endless resources and choices available to you, with more becoming available all the time.

Keep in mind you always have choices in your journey. You make the choice to start and you make the choice to stop. I heard a saying recently that went something like this, "You are only one choice away from a different life."

Remember, Rome wasn't built in a day. Take a deep breath, choose a tool, and jump in! You've got this!

Table of Contents

About the Title, How Are the Humans Winning? 1

Chapter 1 – My Red Light Moment 5

Chapter 2 – Snow Globe 9

Chapter 3 – Beaten but Not Defeated, A Rebel Arises 21

Chapter 4 – The Beginning of a Journey 26

Chapter 5 – Shattered and Broken................................... 28

Chapter 6 – Family Done Differently 42

Chapter 7 – The "T" Word................................... 47

Chapter 8 – Secure Your Mask First 58

Chapter 9 – Dancing in the Dining Room 73

Chapter 10 – Beyond Childhood Trauma 80

Chapter 11 – Burn the Boats 83

Chapter 12 – My Coaching Experience – Sticks and Stones 97

Chapter 13 – Finding Balance and Happiness 102

Chapter 14 – Laundry Chute 107

Chapter 15 – Sammy........................... 113

Chapter 16 – Your Place of Peace 122

Chapter 17 – The Gift of Awareness – Making the Unconscious Conscious................................ 126

Chapter 18 – Random Acts of Self-Kindness That You Never Knew You Were Doing................................ 129

Chapter 19 – Thoughts About Faith and Intuition 133

Chapter 20 – Make Change Normal 136

Chapter 21 – The Sacred Journey 141

Be Your Own Butterfly 146

Ignite Your Inner Rebel 147

Rebel Resources 148

About My Book's Title, How Are the Humans Winning?

We live in an unprecedented time of information, technology, and human connectedness. There has never been a time when virtually anything we want to discover is at our fingertips. Being over fifty, I've had a front row seat to the evolution of technology where we now have 24/7/365 access to information about anything and everything instantly. We can even find a live webcam somewhere in Africa to watch the animals or see crashing waves at a beach on some exotic island. By the same token, we can find any person, organization, or tool we believe can help end our suffering. Any day. Anytime. Anywhere. Thus, the humans are winning!

In contrast, I'm also familiar with having only three TV stations available to watch, with the requirement to walk to the TV to change the channel manually. The phone was attached to the kitchen wall. I knew what it was like to look for a printed dictionary every time someone said a word I didn't understand. Remember, Google was still a long way off in the future.

Now in this information age, we humans have the world stuffed into our pocket or purse in the form of a cell phone. In his comedy special, "Straight, White, Male 60," comedian Dana Carvey had a bit where he was trying to explain to John Lennon the concept of the "miniature computer" everyone carries in a pocket. Just think how attending a video conference with participants all over the world is now considered routine, not marveled at for the brilliance that it is. This is just more evidence that humans are winning.

It's my hope that as I explain my journey of healing and the modalities that helped me along the way as I grew, shifted, and changed, you'll get to know yourself better rather than know me better. What I've learned may help you in your situation and to find what resonates with you and what doesn't.

Another benefit I hope comes from all of this is that you begin to pay close attention to and trust your uniquely human intuition. It's about being willing to listen to the little voice inside of you. That's what might give you tingles when you hear something that really resonates with you or churns your stomach slightly when you hear something that doesn't. I hope you reach a point where you begin to experience and interact with those sensations to allow them to help direct you toward the next right place or state in your life. And be grateful that there are many people and resources in the world to help as you continue to shape your journey.

As we move forward through this book, we'll talk about the array of places, people, services, and modalities that have influenced my life in the past ten years. Note that I do this with the intent of presenting how various influences contribute to our journeys. There's no one option that can serve as a magical cure or solution to change and correct everything in our lives.

Also, it's important to understand when starting any type of healing journey we are our own primary healers and advocates. We are the ones who must fight the hardest for ourselves, our health, our happiness, our peace, our goals, our sovereignty, and even our humanity.

Recognize that, as self-healers, we drive our own healing journeys. As your own personal healer, you'll be partnering with many people and different types of modalities along the way. Some people will help and others won't align with the direction you need to go. In the same way, some of the books and articles you read will resonate with you, while other materials will feel as though they just don't make sense.

At each step, you'll find something that does resonate. There'll be a part of you that will grow. A part of you will blossom. And you'll be energized to find the actions and thinking in life that work for you on your next steps. Think of every experience as a tool in your healing toolkit.

With each book you read, each coach, each class, or each retreat, you can feel gratitude for the tools you pick up along the way. These tools will continue to serve you. Some may involve learning things you don't want to know or having experiences that don't resonate with you. In this collective experience, you'll begin to carve out the path of your unique journey.

I've found that the tools and process cannot and should not be dictated by someone outside of you. Other people can help by mentoring you or pointing you in certain directions. Yet, they cannot do the work for you. They cannot heal you. And they definitely cannot give you an answer that's going permanently end your suffering. This is your journey, your healing, your work to be done. It's about being human.

Therefore, the journey we'll take together will highlight experiences, people, and modalities that I've used at very specific, pivotal times to help me turn different corners and where I have discovered different perspectives. These are the influences that ultimately changed the trajectory of my life. And again, it's my hope that by the end of this book you'll understand yourself, your triggers, and your behavior patterns better. In other words, you'll get to know yourself at a much deeper level. And along with that understanding, you'll feel a deeper love and stronger compassion for yourself. You'll better understand that the people around you are having their own unique experience and I hope you'll have more compassion for what they're likely experiencing on the inside.

I sincerely hope that you can start, or continue, your own journey of healing and also come to acknowledge that The Humans Are Winning… so you too can be a part of the movement.

Chapter 1
My Red Light Moment

Staring forward waiting for a green arrow, I heard the voice on the radio tell a joke and I burst out laughing. Hearing the sound of my own laughter sent a lightning bolt through my entire body. I hadn't laughed in, well, too long to recall.

It was as if the world stopped. It felt like forever between the stoplight's red and green arrows. My laughter sounded foreign to me. That revelation in and of itself wouldn't be such a big deal, except I'm known for my laughter. My colleagues used to tease me that my laugh could be heard across the entire floor. Anyway, my mind was flooded with questions. How did I of all people get to a place where I couldn't even recall laughing? In that same split second, I realized how I desperately missed my laugh. Then came the realization there was no joy in my life. In fact, there was no joy anywhere in my entire world.

As I continued my errands and in the days that followed, it became clear that to regain my laughter, not to mention peace of mind and any hope for my future, I'd have to change everything in my life. Surprisingly, the need for a drastic change didn't shock me. Deep down there was a sense of knowing that the only way to move my life forward was to start over, completely.

Think of this moment as watching an enormous arrangement of dominos that have been intricately laid out and someone has just tapped the first domino. Now imagine that each of these dominos represented a part of my life. This was an entire life review. Not only was I not happy at home, but I also was unhappy at work. I was unhappy with my physical condition and my mental health. My friendships had either ended or were under considerable pressure because of my state of mind at the time. There wasn't a single domino that represented something good in my life. As the enormity of the misery in my life came into clear focus, so too did the understanding that my entire life would need to be burned down in order for a brand-new life to emerge.

My first step was to address the loneliness and isolation that I'd been feeling. I had already been considering adopting a dog, so that seemed like a place to begin. After visiting nearly a dozen shelters looking for the right dog, I found Charlie. He's a poodle and Maltese mix. He and his brother, called Butch and Cassidy by the shelter, were in a tiny room together.

I walked in and sat between them. These two little white fur balls had been found on the side of a road, abandoned by their owner. I knew I could only take one of them, so I was glad there was another family right behind me wanting to see the other puppy.

In the 10 years I've spent with Charlie since that day at the shelter, he has become my little white polar bear, with the heart of a lion and willing to protect me from anything! To say that Charlie changed—dare I say saved—my life in many ways would be a remarkable understatement. In the time after my red light moment, I'd say Charlie has been the one who has given me a reason to put my feet on the ground every day and keep moving forward.

To begin to understand what creating a fresh start in my life might look like, I knew I needed to go directly to the quietest part of me that I had lost touch with. I have many different terms for it now, but at that time I just told myself that I was seeking my intuition, my inner voice. I had silenced the warning signals from by body during some important life decisions and each time I had come to regret not having listened to my inner wisdom. You see, at that time I had only recognized my intuition through sensations in my body.

When I was searching for a dog, I knew I would "feel it" when I found the right one. I'm afraid of large dogs, so I knew my dog had to be a smaller breed. I also wanted the dog to walk and run with me so I wouldn't be looking for a miniature breed either. As soon as I sat down in the room with Charlie and his brother, I felt the way Charlie interacted with me was exactly what I'd been looking for. In that way I "knew" as soon as I locked eyes with him that he was coming home with me. That was my first big step forward.

For some time, prior to my red-light moment, it had been become evident my marriage was not working. Neither of us were happy, our lives were going in different directions, and the friction was increasing to a point where my health was suffering. I was in a situation, an environment, that wasn't good for me and that needed to change. I needed a plan.

Within about six months of my red light moment, after separating from my husband, Charlie and I moved into an apartment. Our new place was within walking distance of my job, so this meant I could get back home during lunch to see Charlie. Happily, the apartment was far enough distance from where I'd been living that I felt like I was gaining some space from my previous life.

Once I settled into the apartment, I knew I needed to start digging into why, at my age, I was living in an apartment, in the process of my third divorce, and feeling defeated. I had always been the eternal optimist. Even after being divorced for the third time, I still deeply believed in marriage. I had been described by people as the person who could fill up a room with my presence and laughter. Yet here I was starting over, again! I was angry, scared, and lost. I knew I needed to do something radically different this time. I promised myself I wouldn't end up in this condition again. I'd do the work to figure out what I was doing to bring the situations, relationships, etc. into my life that kept recreating the trauma of my childhood.

I had absolutely no idea where to begin other than adopting Charlie, nor did I have any indication of just how life-changing my red light moment was to be. Now, 10 years later I look back at that moment and I'm astonished at how different my life is today and how different I am today.

Chapter 2
Snow Globe

The day I moved into my new apartment the poor woman who was working in the office had to deal with me in my not-so-ideal state of mind. I went to the office to get the keys and was sobbing so hard it was difficult for me to even talk, let alone explain what I was doing. She felt bad for me even though she didn't understand why I was crying so hard. Her kindness and that of the movers who helped put everything inside was much appreciated.

I was an absolute mess that day. I don't know if I ever stopped crying. It's interesting to think back about why I was crying so hard. On one level, the tears were a celebration of liberty. I was leaving what had become a toxic relationship that was moving in a very dark direction. On another level, I was in anguish that I had another failed marriage.

Having a stable, happy marriage and homelife was a deep desire of mine. Yet, up to that point I had been incapable of creating a lasting relationship. My relationships would be good for about two years, then they'd begin to fall apart. It took some relationships longer to go in the wrong direction than others, but eventually they became unsustainable. They all fell apart for roughly the same reasons. The inner dialogue of the relationships became strained, then angry, and then cruel. That's when I would leave.

Was I going to be able to change that dynamic or was I now destined to be alone? Thank heavens for Charlie, having him there gave me the courage and strength to keep moving.

Thinking back, maybe I was sobbing due to the enormity of what I intuitively knew was about to happen—the complete unraveling of all the childhood and adult trauma I had experienced. There was no more suppressing it or pretending I was fine or that I had moved beyond my past. The truth was there, with no place left for it to go. It was time to start honestly facing my life, myself. Who was I? Whom did I want to be? Where did I want to go? How did I want to live? For any of us, these are incredibly intimidating, big questions.

Granted, I've asked myself these questions many times over my life. Yet this time somehow there was a different depth to it. At this stage of my life there was a sense of urgency. I knew the changes I was making this time were going to be ones that would direct my future. There was no going back!

Poor Charlie was so exhausted from the chaotic day, he'd passed out on the floor. I was equally drained from the emotional upheaval and just running on adrenaline. As I looked around my apartment I thought, "What now? Where to begin?" This is what I refer to as a snow globe moment.

Perhaps this is true for everyone, but I've found when I make any life change it's as if my life is suddenly turned upside down and shaken in ways that every corner of my life is affected. Some might say that's the nature of change, but in my experience even the smallest shift I've made had compound effects on my life. Of course, when you're on the precipice of divorce, your entire world is going to be upended.

As I stood in the center this snow globe experience, I felt as if all the pieces of my life were floating around me. I closed my eyes and thought, "Okay I'm here. What the hell do I do now?"

I'd begun all the paperwork to end my marriage. As part of that process, a friend's stepfather, a financial planner, helped me sort through my financial issues. This included getting my debts under control and making a plan to become financially stable and secure. During one of our conversations, he suggested that I work with a life coach and recommended someone to me. That sounded like a reasonable step to start settling at least some aspects of my new life.

Working with this first life coach turned out to be a disappointing experience because I didn't feel supported at all. I wasn't given strategies for how I could work with my demons or how to develop new ways to behave and respond to life events. There was never a plan, even to answer the simple question: "What are we working on?" Much of the time was spent talking about what was happening in my coach's traumatic life. The one benefit I did get from this coaching engagement was to become aware of the book by Brené Brown, *The Gifts of Imperfection*. Still the optimist!

This book was a complete paradigm changer for me. Here was someone who was writing about insecurities and the way we see ourselves. This was my initial foray into the self-help world and Brown's book served as a spark for change. Knowing what I know now, I acknowledge that this spark could just as easily have been from an article, video, speech, conversation, or experience. I'm not sure we know what the spark will be until we've felt the impact. That's why it's important to always keep an open mind because your spark of inspiration may come from an unlikely source.

After reading Brown's book, I started to have some real aha moments about the beliefs that had been projected on me by family, friends, and even business associates. The beliefs I'd adopted as my own had become part of my personality and what I thought of myself. That book helped me I realize that I needed to start making my well-being a priority and begin forming my own beliefs about myself. One change was that I became much more curious about my opinions. Where did they come from? Are they even what I believe anymore?

A couple areas that I began to pay closer attention to included my speech and my reactions. Part of this was to be able to ask myself if the reactions I'd become accustomed to were based on my own beliefs, were they just habitual, or from external sources. I started to feel a much more profound shift in my thinking as I started to question my own beliefs, my own responses, my own patterns. Where did all this come from? Was any of this actually me? What was genuine for me? And who was this persona behind the patterns and beliefs that had been built over time for understandable reasons at different times in my life?

Parents and caregivers imprint behavior patterns on their children. It's usually done unknowingly because those patterns are in the unconscious. It's critical to understand just how deeply childhood patterns can continue to affect us long into our adult lives.

An example of imprinted behavior patterns is consistently having an elevated stress level that we may not even be aware of. After being under stress for so long, that state of mind and body can become normal. It can shift us into a mode of being constantly reactive as though we're in danger all the time. Having an elevated stress level is also dangerous for the body. When the body is in fight, flight, or freeze mode, many of the bodily systems don't function properly, which can lead to all sorts of health issues.

For me, this stress affected all aspects of my life, in particular my ability to sleep. Since I was working full time, I knew I had to get some decent sleep so I could be clearheaded and productive at work. Another health pattern, related to stress was migraines. There were times when I would experience migraines for multiple days. I wouldn't be able to work, eat, or sleep.

This realization about the state of my mind and body led me to start asking myself a lot of questions while doing my best to be patient even when frustrated due to not finding any answers. I felt as a grown woman I should be able to figure out these things. However, at the same time I'd never had training to do anything like this. Just knowing how to survive didn't equip me to know how to perform such deep self-analysis and launch massive changes in my life. While I knew how to find a job, feed myself, and survive, I needed to figure out the aspects of my life that were most important for me to change. What should I start working on immediately to feel the biggest positive impact?

I started asking myself the hard questions like, "What do I want?," I wasn't asking what I wanted to be when I grew up. It was more along the lines of, "What do I want my daily life to look like?" or "What do I want my job to be like?" or "What do I want my next relationship to look like?"

Even though I hadn't had stellar luck with relationships in terms of marriage, I still deeply believed in the institution of marriage. I believe in that bond between two people and a desire to spend the rest of their lives together. And I understood how two people could resonate on a level that worked for them to experience those feelings. I still held that belief about marriage and I still wanted to experience that in my life.

Now, I needed to know what getting better even meant. Would that be about feeling better? Would that mean all those childhood memories would disappear? I think it can be scary to not know what comes next. I knew what I had in my life up until that moment standing in the apartment wasn't working. At the same time I knew how I wanted my life to look. What I didn't know was how to get from where I was to where I wanted to be. I had no foundation beneath me, so there really wasn't anything to hold on to for stability.

Standing inside the snow globe with every part of my life floating around me was overwhelming. I was looking at each flake and trying to determine what was mine, what was imprinted on me, and if I needed to keep it. Did I need to put parts of my life away, fix them, or heal them? And what did healing even mean? How would I get there and how would I know if I got there? There were so many questions, I felt like my head might explode.

I remained determined that this time would be different. I knew therapy wouldn't work and the coaching had left me feeling uninspired, so I decided to find a path based on intuition. It was clear that a critical piece of this journey was to get back in touch with myself and my intuition, so working with a professional intuitive made sense to me. I asked around in my network of contacts for a referral and was introduced to a wonderfully talented woman, whom I still work with ten years later.

During our first meeting, I was paying close attention to how my body was responding to the information she was sharing with me. It was important to make sure whatever changes I made in my life were for the right reasons and lasting. I didn't want temporary fixes. Leading up to the meeting with the intuitive I sat by myself and quietly thought about how the same types of situations and relationships kept showing up in my life like patterns. It was recognizing the patterns that most encouraged and intimidated me at the same time.

On one hand, recognizing the patterns is half the battle. At least you're now aware that patterns are part of the issue. Since most patterns are unconscious, often you've acted out the pattern before even noticing it's going to happen. That was the intimidating part. If I'm only witnessing the patterns after the damage is done, how am I going to change those patterns?

The intuitive helped me confirm the need for major changes in my life. She also left me with a profound insight. She explained that the universe would attempt to guide me toward my path, gently at first. However, if I'm not getting the message and making the necessary adjustments the universe would send a stronger message to help remind me to listen to myself and follow my heart.

The case she gave was with people who work too much, even though they know it's damaging their performance, health, and relationships. They either don't want to slow down or don't know how to break from their jobs to create more balance in their lives. Perhaps they're involved in an accident or contract a disease. Then by their circumstances they're forced to slow down and create more balanced lives. Often in hindsight those individuals recognize they'd ignored the signs, even though the signals were all around them. That was until they were forced to acknowledge them.

To put this point another way, Jai Dev Singh from Life Force Academy says that when there are tensions in your life, meet them and work with them. In this way you're facing those situations and resolving them versus ignoring them and having them surface in more challenging ways.

I hadn't been following my intuition and certainly not following my heart for a very long time. I was in a place of deep unhappiness, loneliness, and isolation. Frankly, I had been in survival mode for all of my life. I'd ignored all the warning signs about where I was headed. So, it was tremendously helpful to have someone confirm what my intuition was telling me needed to be changed in and about my life.

It was clear that there was much work for me to do. It would take time for the different parts of my life to settle in very different ways than they'd been in the past. The fact is that many aspects of my life are still settling into place. I suppose a certain amount of snow globe shaking is just part of life for all of us. I knew that to start settling things and claim any level of happiness or joy and any true peace, I just needed to take a first step. Any step would do.

In addition to taking care of Charlie, I knew I needed to take better care of myself by healing my heart. My divorce and difficult personal history caused me a tremendous amount of emotional pain. It was unsettling to face how I was so overdue to come to terms with everything that had happened to me in my life. I was only beginning to understand how the events from my childhood were still affecting me.

Since I'm an energetic person with a lot of fire in my astrology chart, I felt some type of physical activity would be the best place for me to start. It would help me work through my energy and calm me. It also might present me with the opportunity to start feeling better about myself—having a kinder, gentler opinion of myself.

That's when I decided to hire a personal trainer as a next step in my new journey. The trainer came to my apartment three mornings a week and I worked out for an hour before heading off to my job. This physical activity turned out to be an amazingly fabulous, positive decision. The more I worked out, the more I felt like I was taking back my life, taking back my body, and taking back my time. I was building strength in my body. I also was building self-confidence and self-esteem. The workouts helped me transform my feelings of being powerless to feelings of being powerful. I began embracing the act of regaining control over my physical health and through that my mental health. When I exercised vigorously, I felt much lighter. Interestingly, I felt it was easier for me to deal with projects at work with a clearer mind because I had more energy and didn't feel so heavy all the time.

From this one decision and action, I came to understand something very important about myself. It's that I felt much better when I had a lot of movement in my life, when I was physically expressing myself more and building strength in my body. This may be obvious to many, but at that time it wasn't obvious to me. I found it to be a transformative experience.

For perspective, some people who read that may think it's obvious that exercise is going to give you more energy and more clarity. I'd like to point out that children who are severely abused haven't necessarily been exposed to mundane day-to-day life activities. Using exercise to illustrate this is that no one in my family ever discussed exercise as a way to feel better or improve our health. I exercised at school and played sports, as required, but I never connected movement with physical or mental health. There's an innocence, or ignorance, to adults who have merely survived their life where seemingly obvious things are a mystery.

My work with the personal trainer made me feel like I'd begun to take substantive steps to move myself forward to a place where I could begin to feel organic joy. I was taking ownership of the experience of physical activity and, thereby, ownership of my life. There was joy in the choices I was making because I knew I was making them for myself and to improve my life. I felt like every day I was taking another step toward a better future and movement toward a little bit more hope.

I began to celebrate my taking the time to understand where I needed to be in my life. I was starting to see the results of deciding what was good and not good for me. This affected all areas of my life, including friendships in and outside my profession, my daily self-care, and how I connected with society. I even took ownership of things like what news I watched and what radio stations I listened to. Along the way I found it was important for me to start paying attention to the outside influences I was feeding myself.

It's important to remember how everything that comes into our sensory perception affects us. It changes us to some degree and certainly influences our behavior. We need to take ownership of which external influences we open ourselves to and what each decision means.

There were other surprising outcomes from my take-charge approach. One unusual change I made was to stop watching football. I'd watched professional football from about the age of five. I was a true fan. Those exciting Monday and Thursday night games helped break up the week. But one of the choices I made in the early days at my new apartment was to stop watching football. Why? I suddenly looked at the game through the eyes of a person who couldn't stand violence. I also didn't like the tension of the game, in the stands or on social media. The players and coaches have become larger than life in stature. Such athletes exert an outsized influence on the people who follow them. I didn't like how those athletes were affecting me. That needed to end.

Letting go of football illustrates the depth of change I embraced. It wasn't just about getting a new haircut, finding a new boyfriend, or reading a book about change. I began a deep and ongoing transformation, including how it related to the people I chose to see and be with.

It's important to consider the people you welcome into your life and how deeply influential they are as you move along your journey. How well do they and other resources you engage resonate with you? Do you feel as though they provide the opportunity to improve your situation? Most importantly, do these people give you more information that you can use to support your efforts to settle the swirl of floating aspects of life, in your snow globe? It's all about making choices.

One thing had become abundantly clear to me by this point. It was that the roots of my suffering were a long way back in my childhood. The issues to be solved were not of the here and now; they were of the past. And that was where I needed to travel to resolve them.

I'd like to add a thought about the importance of celebrating the small things along the way in a journey of healing. About four months after I moved into my apartment, I had what I call my big exhale. I was lying on the couch after dinner, the show Downton Abbey was on the TV and Charlie was on the floor playing with a toy when I felt… joy. There was no crisis, no threat of violence. I could breathe and feel like I was finally safe and in a good place. It wasn't that I had all the answers nor a comprehensive plan for moving forward. In a way I didn't need that so much. What I did need was to recognize this elusive feeling of peace and joy. That moment was confirmation for me that I was moving in the right direction with my life.

Such private little celebrations become the moments that empower you and give you the strength and courage to keep moving forward when you feel like you have nothing left to give.

Chapter 3
Beaten but Not Defeated, a Rebel Arises

I stood there in the bathroom shaking, crying, and bleeding. Staring directly into the eyes of the monster who had just done this to me she said, "I did this to you because I love you."

As far as trauma goes, that's where the memory ends. People don't understand when you're exposed to a deeply traumatic experience, your memories may never be clear or sequential. Memories and perhaps sensations come in flashes or bits and pieces. Equally, it can take years for the memories to surface, which can be traumatizing on its own.

Now looking back, I think one of the most remarkable things about that whole situation was this seven-year-old girl who understood at her core that everything this woman was saying was wrong. Knowing this behavior couldn't be the definition of love. It was terror, brutality. There was zero evidence of love.

So, why was it necessary for me to understand the importance of keeping secrets? What secret didn't I keep? What did I do to earn this brutality? I'll fill you in on that pivotal time in my life.

I was about seven, living in Arizona with my mother, brother, sister, and stepfather. At the time, we had a cousin staying with us. On this particular day, several members of my extended family were at our house helping my stepfather. There were two or three uncles, plus four or five male cousins and my grandmother. The older kids were in middle school, and I was in second grade so I was always home early. My sister, brother, and I shared a large adjoining room. I would wait on my brother's bed and watch for them because his side of the room had a whole wall of windows that faced the front of the house.

While I waited impatiently for them to come home from school, I laid on his bed and colored. That's when a car sped up to the front of the house and slid to a stop on the dirt driveway. Dust and rocks flew everywhere. I was startled because I'd never seen anyone arrive this way.

Less than a minute later I heard my mother start screaming, "I need to get my baby. I need to get my baby." Suddenly, the door flew open. My mother rushed forward, followed closely by a man with a mask over his face. He was pointing a gun at her. She scooped me up and carried me into the foyer. I saw all my relatives lying face down on the foyer floor with their hands tied behind their backs. As we came into the foyer, I noticed there were men all around the room, in every corner and they were all armed. The masked gunman sat my mother down on a couch and put me on the floor between her legs. Directly in front of me were my grandmother's feet, as she lay bound on the floor.

It's important to understand that if anyone asked my siblings or me what my stepfather did for a living, we were told to say he was in the wholesale jewelry business, selling turquoise. The truth? He was a marijuana dealer. He kept dozens of large green garbage bags full of marijuana around the house. I remember thinking they looked somewhat like bales of hay.

It was obvious these men either wanted the drugs or money, or both. I'm still unclear about what they were after. At some point, they took my stepfather down the hallway. When he returned, he had my sister's sweater draped over his head and there was blood dripping down from it.

Things were very tense and there was a lot of shouting. I don't recall what they were yelling about. The ringleader stood behind my mother, shouting, and asking questions. He stepped forward and said if no one was going to cooperate, then they'd just take me on the road with them for their entertainment.

At that point, I blacked out. I didn't faint. I simply went into such deep shock that I have no recollection of anything else that happened. The next thing I remember, the masked men were all gone. All my relatives were trying to determine how bad my stepfather's head injury was from being hit with the butt of a gun.

Moments later, my brother, sister, and cousin came home from school. I ran outside to tell them what had happened. Because I was a young child, they didn't believe me. They walked into the house and were astonished by the chaos.

I'd never seen any guns in the house prior to this event. Afterward, the house was loaded with guns... everywhere. They were placed behind curtains and doors. It was terrifying. I don't know what would have happened if bad guys had invaded our house again or if a family member became totally irrational or enraged at someone.

I went to school the next day and told a friend that our house had gotten broken into. As I relayed the ordeal, I made sure to include the cover story of my parent's jewelry business.

That night, my friend had a nightmare about what I'd told her and told her father about it. After he comforted her, he called my parents to find out if he could be of any assistance. Unbeknownst to me, he was a police officer.

The details of the conversation weren't revealed to me except that he called to make sure everyone was okay and offered to write a report or help identify what had been stolen. I recall my mother taking my brother and sister into the bedroom along with my stepfather to talk while I was getting ready to go to bed. A couple minutes later, my mother took me into the bedroom with everyone and proceeded to ask me what I had said to my friend at school.

I recounted what I'd said. My memory of what happened next is a bit fuzzy, but I do remember my mom looking at my brother and sister saying, "You should watch what's about to happen because this will be what's going to happen to you if I find out that you've told anyone."

She proceeded to beat the hell out of me. She gouged both sides of my neck with her fingernails and snapped a belt at me as I tried to run from her, causing welts up and down my body. She ripped out both my ponytails and the night-shirt I had been wearing was torn and bloody.

I don't know how long this beating went on. What I do remember is standing in the bathroom with my sister sitting in front of me sobbing, asking me to be quiet and to stop crying.

All the while she wiped the blood off my face and tried to clean me up.

It was at that point my mother walked in and pushed my sister aside. She got down on her knees inches away from me and looked me directly in the eyes. She explained that she'd done this because she loved me. She said she needed me to understand that when something was a secret, it was to remain a secret. And with that, she left.

I'd been beaten so badly that no part of me wasn't bruised, swollen, or bleeding. The next week I wasn't allowed to go to school or anywhere in public.

Why did this occur? More importantly, why am I sharing this traumatic experience with you? It's because I've spent a tremendous amount of time unwinding the damage of child abuse and the terror that I experienced. So much of my life fundamentally changed when my mother knelt before me and said she'd beaten me because she loved me.

That moment is embedded in my unconscious. There has been much talk about how 90 percent of individuals' lives is run by their unconscious, through behavior patterns and belief systems. We make so many decisions without even thinking about why we made them or if they made any sense. Through my self-discovery journey it has become clear there were many patterns and beliefs formed in that moment with my mother and the rest of my family.

In hindsight, my mother planted the seeds of my independence and ignited my rebellious nature in that exchange. It didn't begin as a healthy independence, though. Instead, I felt completely alone and started believing there was no one I would ever be able to trust. I understood there was no one willing to protect me.

Chapter 4
The Beginning of a Journey

A consequence of these experiences was that I believed I could not count on anyone because no one protected me. Of course, now it makes sense that nobody in my home would've protected me or anyone else. But to my child self, it was traumatic that no one stood up for me. The person who is supposed to care about me the most was my abuser and she was the one who did this to me. It's perfectly natural I would create a belief about being unsafe. A secondary belief was also created, which was the only person I was ever going to be able to count on was myself.

At the time in my childhood, these were valid beliefs. I wasn't safe. I wasn't loved. I wasn't protected. And I wouldn't be protected by any of the people who lived in my home, ever. The larger implication was that those experiences produced my inability to trust anybody. One's family, or care givers, are at the core of a child's belief systems regarding trust, love, caring, safety, and nurturing. Destroying those beliefs has lifelong implications.

My life from that point on was built on this new belief system. The end consequence was believing that I could only count on myself to survive. It took me years to unwind all of this. I came to understand that one experience created behavioral patterns that were so deep they'd have had significant effects on my everyday life thereafter. These behaviors debilitated all my relationships and interactions with others, no matter if they were friends, colleagues, or lovers.

If I had more resources when I was growing up, I would have been better able to defend and protect myself. Maybe I wouldn't have felt like I couldn't trust anyone, and no one could love me.

But that wasn't the case in my childhood. Since then, I've come to realize that there often are layers of others' patterns thrust upon us from youth and onward. When these layers are removed, we can come closer to being our genuine selves. We'll be able to operate from a place of self-sovereignty, one that's built upon our own beliefs and patterns. Doing this will help us establish our own sense of direction based on who we are, who we want to be, and where we want to go.

Chapter 5
Shattered and Broken

I was lying in bed knowing full well that I wouldn't be able to sleep that night. It was the end of what probably was the worst day of my life. I was 15 at the time and had been dating my boyfriend for about a year or year and a half.

In many ways, until that night, he was kind of the perfect first serious boyfriend to have. Even though he was five years older, I never felt as though I needed to do anything to please him. Maybe it was because he'd been one of my brother's best friends so I'd known him for quite some time.

Around the time my mother and stepfather were divorcing, my mother didn't have a place to live so I'd gone to live with a school friend for several months to have some stability in my life. Once my mother found a man to live with, I returned to be with them and my brother. That's when the nature of my relationship with my boyfriend changed.

He was very sweet and gentle. Never pushing, controlling, or making lewd suggestive comments about having sex, since I was a virgin. Very early in our relationship he assured me that it would be my decision and he'd respect that however long it took. Although, after several months I wanted to move to that level in our relationship. I was grateful for how he treated me and appreciate it even to this day.

My eventual introduction to sex was in a beautiful, wonderful relationship with this person whom I truly believed loved me. I truly loved him. The fact that I was so young was immaterial to me.

I'd been forced to abandon my childhood due to my chaotic and dangerous family. The adults in my life had exposed me to a different type of sexual behavior. My mother and stepfather routinely had sex with their bedroom door open and openly in other areas of the house. They never seemed to notice how their behavior was affecting everyone else in the house.

When I experienced sex for the first time, I didn't feel too young. I felt like it was a very natural progression in a relationship. It wasn't a one-night stand, like for many teenage girls who after prom were pressured into having sex. This was a loving, mutually meaningful relationship. I believe I'm more capable of having good, trusting, physical intimacy with my husband now because of the gentle way sexual intimacy was introduced into my life. Looking back I can say I was too young, but at the time it didn't feel that way.

This fabulous loving relationship made me want to have a different life than my family's. The mutual respect, gentleness, and love I felt gave me hope. It made me believe that I could actually achieve something better.

My boyfriend's homelife was radically different from mine. He came from an affluent background. His family was nice. They lived in a lovely home and he and his brother seemed to have all the things that life had to offer.

In contrast, I lived in poverty my whole life. Being exposed to his world was like finding the magic land in the back of the closet as in the C.S. Lewis novel, *The Lion, the Witch, and the Wardrobe*. I realized this kind of life really did exist.

I had decided long ago I didn't want anything to do with the kind of life my family had built or its outcomes. What my boyfriend had was how I wanted my life to look. I wanted to have that nice home. I wanted to have the freedom and flexibility of that life and to enjoy having pretty things around me. Walking into his world was such an eye-opening experience for me. And the fact that he was so loving and kind to me made that all the more special. Our relationship made me want his kind of life even more because of how well he treated me.

At that point in my life, I thought I had my love story. Though my boyfriend and I always used protection whenever we were intimate, I decided to surprise him and get a prescription for birth control pills at Planned Parenthood while he and his brother were on vacation. His birthday was the week after he came back from vacation, so this was one of his "gifts."

Instead of getting a prescription, to my utter and complete astonishment I had a positive pregnancy test. It felt like the walls started closing in on me as the doctor delivered the news. I was in disbelief. How did this happen? We had prided ourselves on being careful. I also started wondering what was I going to do? I was only 15. Oh, my God. I'd have to tell my mother. Oh, my God.

The day started out with me feeling so empowered and a little bit mischievous. Then, it turned into a total catastrophe. What made everything worse was that I had no support from anyone. My brother wasn't around much. He was doing his own thing with his job and circle of friends. My sister wished me luck as she dropped me back at home to tell my mother. I'm sure my sister knew exactly what was coming when I spilled the news.

Well, the showdown with my mother quickly devolved into accusations of what a slut and failure I was. She said I was her last chance at having a good child. More cruel comments and insults followed. Like she often did when she was upset, she left and got drunk. I was left sitting there, asking myself, "What am I going to do?"

In this house, one of the few luxuries I had was my own telephone line in my bedroom. This unusual gift wasn't because my mother was trying to be generous. It was because the house phone line was for her business. I wasn't allowed to use that phone or give out the number to anyone. She gave me my own phone line to get me out of her hair.

Alone in my room, agonizing about my predicament, I was startled when the phone rang at around 1:30 in the morning. On the other end was an unfamiliar female voice. She didn't give her name but asked, "Is this Tawnya?" After I told her it was, the next words out of her mouth broke my heart. She said, "I think you have the right to know that the night before your boyfriend left on vacation, he went to a party. And he had sex with another girl in a hot tub."

I told her that couldn't possibly be true. He'd never do that to me. I rambled on with all the denials one says in a moment like that. Then, she told me the girl's name and identified where the house was. She even named some of the other guests who were there.

The caller then passed the phone to a friend of mine who told me, "She's telling you the truth," and handed the phone back to the caller. I had a million questions, but nothing changed the facts.

Just when I thought the day couldn't get any worse after receiving the news I was pregnant, I got that call. It's an understatement to say that the bottom dropped out of whatever so-called world I'd manufactured around that relationship.

It's impossible to describe the cascading devastation I felt, the betrayal and the utter hopelessness. I had lost my innocence to this man. I'd opened my heart and life to him. And he actually made me start believing that something better in my life was possible. Then he crushed me on every emotional level. I had loved him, but in return he shredded every ounce of trust and love that we'd built. Compounding all this was knowing I was carrying his child.

Added blows came from my mother who told me how she despised me and reinforced I was never going to amount to anything. This was nothing new to me, but now she had a solid example of my recklessness and irresponsibility to point to. I knew she sure as hell wasn't going to hold my hand now. No. In her estimation, I deserved having my boyfriend betray me because I was foolish enough to have allowed myself to have gotten into this situation.

I felt like I was drowning. In the space of 12 hours, I learned I was pregnant, was abandoned and demeaned once again by my mother, forsaken by my family, and learned of my boyfriend's infidelity. The one person I loved and believed loved me had destroyed me. I just sat there asking, "Oh my God. What's going to happen to me now? What am I going to do? How am I going to survive this?"

The next day my mother informed me exactly what I was going to do. She told me what was going to happen, how, when, and where. Because I was 15, I had no legal rights to determine what I wanted to do. She had decided for me that I was going to have an abortion and she did it with glee. She saw it as a golden opportunity to convince me that I was no better than she was and to crush any ambitions and dreams I had. I saw it as just another instance of her incessant cruelty.

The whole thing made my head spin. I was still reeling from the news that I was pregnant and trying to process that. Now I was told I had an appointment to end my pregnancy. And I still hadn't figured out how in the hell I was going to deal with my boyfriend and the fact that he'd cheated on me.

I felt as if I was standing in the middle of a forest fire, uncertain which area to try to put out first. I had no idea what to do, who to talk to, or who to reach out to. There was no support. No one cared. No one listened. It wasn't their problem. I was the young kid who had gotten herself into this tragic situation and shown that she had no ability to make good decisions. My irresponsibility proved it was obvious that someone else needed to make all my decisions for me.

I wondered if anyone wanted to hear my side of this. Was anyone even going to ask me how I was doing? Well, the answer to that question was the answer to all my questions. No.

The cruel irony of this entire situation was that my abortion was scheduled on my boyfriend's birthday. What timing, especially since he was required to attend the procedure. Rather than the welcome home greeting he expected, he learned the uncomfortable news that I was carrying his child and I also knew what he had done the night before he left.

Oddly, I felt a momentary sense of relief that someone else's world was being shaken as hard as mine. But it was only fleeting because I knew I couldn't trust him. He couldn't be my boyfriend, certainly not my friend or support structure. He couldn't be anything I needed.

I was devastated by what he had done and by his defense of his actions. He claimed it was okay to have sex with another girl because it was only physical. There were no feelings involved. That didn't minimize the situation. It just made me angrier that he thought that sentiment would appease me. As I stood there looking at him, I felt like I was standing alone on a deserted island surrounded by the biggest ocean. I was broken, alone, numb with anger… lost.

Then, the reality of all this brought me back to questions I couldn't answer. How the hell would I survive this? My heart was broken. I was being forced to have a procedure that I didn't want. But I didn't know what I wanted. I would've liked to sit down and think about what I wanted. Thanks to my mother, that wasn't a luxury offered to me.

Before I continue, I'm compelled to share my deeply held beliefs about abortion. I believe that a woman who is pregnant is the only human capable of making the decision about whether or not she should have that child. She should have the final word, regardless of what path led her to her pregnancy, be it consensual or non-consensual in any way. That is my fundamental belief about abortion.

That decision about the abortion was stolen from me by my mother as well as by an entire set of other people and organizations. They never gave me the opportunity to speak, to participate in making that life-changing decision. No woman standing on this planet deserves to be treated that way. To think that something so invasive could happen to a woman's body without her consent is abhorrent. It's unacceptable and inflicts a lifetime of emotional damage to the woman.

The day I underwent my abortion, I was whisked into a room and given medication to put me under. When I awoke, my life was fundamentally changed forever. Yet, I awakened to see the kindest eyes I'd ever gazed at. This was a nurse who was looking at me, holding my hand, and crying. I was amazed that there actually was some kindness in the world. Everything up to that moment had been so sharp, cold, and devastating. Finally, someone was looking at me with kindness and compassion. I noticed another person in the room wiping blood off the floor. It was a painful reminder about what just happened. Then, I was moved to a recovery room for a while where I slept. Once I was awake, I was given an examination. Then my mother and my former boyfriend took me home.

My mother required me to sit on the living room couch with everyone else. I wasn't allowed to be alone, go to my room to rest, to cry, or to try to process what had just happened to me. I still was in shock from learning I'd been pregnant and that my boyfriend had betrayed me. Now I was faced with the magnitude of having had a procedure I never consented to and the fact that I was never given a choice to decide what I wanted.

I can only describe my mental state as feeling like everything had been stripped from me, my love relationship, my child, and my freedom. My world was limited to the couch, the kitchen, and the bathroom. And when I was in the bathroom the door had to be open so I could be observed 24 hours a day, seven days a week. This was another cruelty imposed by my mother. She continually reminded me how my recklessness and irresponsibility had put me into this situation and that I only had myself to blame.

All of this wore me down. I had no fight left in me, no hope, no desire to be alive anymore. I just wanted to disappear into the darkness and never have to come back. I was in pain, emotionally and physically. I was filled with mental anguish and horror. All I thought about was that I just wanted to be dead. I didn't want to have to live in this body, in this situation, in this family anymore.

It was impossible to see that I'd have a chance to better myself or have a better life, let alone a loving family and a husband. The perfect fantasy I'd created about the relationship with my former boyfriend had been shattered. I couldn't see past what had happened. There was no way to see around it or through it to the other side.

After a period of punishment, I was finally allowed to sleep in my room. But I had to keep the door open so I could be observed. This didn't last because my mother couldn't put her drinking or carousing on hold forever. One night when she was out drinking, I packed a bag, crawled out my window, climbed over the fence, and ran away.

I didn't run away to a friend's house. Instead, I went to the local police station. When I entered, I told them that I wanted to be taken away from my mother. I wanted to enter into foster care or even an orphanage. It didn't matter where I went, as long as I was away from my mother. I was only 15 at the time, but I knew I had to escape. I didn't believe I could survive living with her for three more years until I was considered a legal adult.

One reason I gave the officers why I wanted to get away from my mother was because she was a cocaine dealer. I told them I could help them arrest her and others with information as to who her supplier was, her customers were, and those she supplied at the bar where she worked. The knowledge I was willing to share with them could have resulted in numerous arrests connected to the drugs on this town's streets.

I knew everything about the business, even who her dealers were and where they lived. Drug deals happened in broad daylight right in front of me my whole life. It started with marijuana only, but quickly expanded during my teen years when my mother and stepfather divorced. My mother went completely off the deep end with drugs and alcohol. Piles of cocaine sat on our living room table all the time.

My meeting at the police station seemed to last for hours. I pleaded with them to help me. In exchange I gave them valuable information about my mother that could allow me to be legally taken away from her. What was odd was that they didn't call anyone, file a report, or do anything. There was no attempt to check the veracity of my story or offer any kind of assistance. To my astonishment, the police put me in the back of a squad car and delivered me right back to my front door.

The officers just dropped me off, like nothing I'd said mattered. They explained to my mother that I'd sought their help to be taken away from her. Though she was very respectful in front of them, I knew the fury behind that façade. I had flashbacks to when I was seven and had told my friend whose father was a policeman that our house had been broken into. I was well aware of how she felt about the police possibly learning about her lifestyle and "business."

In the officers' eyes, my mother couldn't possibly be the horribly violent, toxic woman whom I described. I must just be a spoiled child who didn't get my way and decided to run to the police. That's how they made me feel. Not safe, not heard, not seen. I thought if I couldn't go to law enforcement and deliver a cocaine dealer then my life truly was meaningless.

I knew as soon as the police left, all hell was going to break loose. I wondered how our confrontation would end. One of us was going to have to give, although, I didn't know how much more I could give. I'd just had my body pillaged, my trust betrayed, and my whole world shattered. I didn't have anything left. I didn't care anymore. Whatever my mother was going to do, she was going to do. I had no one left to call for help knowing that the police had just delivered me back to the person who was actively trying to destroy my life.

I didn't know my situation could get even darker. After she closed the door, she became scarily quiet for a little bit. She looked down at me and said, "I learned from *Mommie Dearest* that if you wrap a coat hanger in a towel, you can beat someone to death with it and it won't leave any bruises. They won't be able to tell how you died because there'll be so much internal damage."

She said this frightening, vicious thing to me as calm as could be. I figured she was beyond rage at that point. I looked at her and I said, "Great, how long is that going to take? Should I get the coat hanger for you? Should I wrap it for you? What kind of towel do we need? And you said a wire coat hanger? A wooden hanger would work faster. Don't we have any better weapons in the house or is it mainly important that there be no external bruises? I mean, obviously, the police don't give a shit what you do to me. They just drove away and left me with you."

She just looked at me. I was dumbfounded and said, "Don't you get it? You win. You win. Because if you beat me to death, if you shoot me, if you stab me, whatever you do to get rid of me, that means I'll never have to spend another second with you. And isn't that what this is all about now? Getting away from you. You should be pleased. I've disappointed you. I've let you down. Look how I failed you. This is the next obvious step. You win. How can I help you carry this out?"

As she looked at me, I honestly couldn't read the emotion on her face. All she said was," I truly despise you." She turned around and walked out of the house.

That time—after the pregnancy, the betrayal of my boyfriend, the forced abortion, plus the cruelty and punishment of my mother—were some of the darkest, bleakest, most hopeless days of my entire life. No cliche fits, such as, "Those events made me stronger" or "That which doesn't kill you makes you stronger."

Thankfully, six to eight months after that incident with my mother, just past my sixteenth birthday, I was given the opportunity to never have to live with her again.

I'm fairly convinced that something about that abortion damaged my body to the point that I was never able to carry another child. So, my mother took another thing from me. She took my childhood. She took my adolescence. And then by forcing me to have that procedure, she took my ability to be a mother away from me. On top of all this, she never told me who my real father was. She kept his identity from me and took it to her grave.

I find it difficult to forgive some of those things. Nevertheless, I will say that those experiences were indicators of the resilience and the strength that I had and still possess. Resilience and self-reliance were my survival lifelines. There were no resources available other than what was inside of me. I had no county resources, society resources, family resources, or friend resources. Somehow my strength and resilience saw me through all that.

As I sit here looking back at those situations, I'm humbled by that young woman's strength, my strength. I'm humbled because those were truly life altering situations happening to a 15-year-old child. She navigated her way through all that to come out the other side still capable of loving other people, able to form relationships, and desiring for many years to be a mother. That is until age and other factors determined the mother part wasn't going to happen.

I suppose in retrospect, if there were ever going to be one true heartbreak of my life, it would be that I never held a child in my arms to whom I gave birth. This is the greatest heartbreak of my life.

Over the years, I've faced the consequences of those two situations and how they've shaped my decisions and relationships over the course of my life. I've finally learned how to give myself compassion, kindness, tenderness, and loads and loads of love and understanding. Certainly, there still are some sticky bits about my past for me even now. But I understand those sticky bits better now. I can make room for them when they come up and can understand where they're coming from. That way, I don't project them out into my life or onto my husband or anywhere else. I simply understand that they're echoes of very deep, transformational, hard situations that I experienced.

If you've ever had your personal sovereignty taken from you in the ways I've experienced or by abuse of some other sort, you understand there's a lot of work to be done that involves trust and setting boundaries. Furthermore, there may be parts of your trauma that can surprise you at times.

I find these surprises may be triggered by memories that come out of nowhere. Maybe a chaotic situation that happened in my childhood pops into my head. Usually, I can hold my equilibrium through those flashbacks. Sometimes I can't. There are times when they knock me off my routine or my normal state for a few days. This is when I focus on bringing some kindness and compassion to myself and my life to allow those feelings to be healed.

I urge you to allow your wisdom to release the pain so you can continue moving forward. It's that ongoing, unfolding process that we go through as we heal from situations that have happened in our lives. Try not to compare them to the level of drama or trauma in others' lives. Yours could be one event or possibly a host of events that when woven together created the patterns or beliefs around your experience. It's a process. Learn to be present each day, with yourself and with those around you. Each of us has had a unique constellation of events that has brought us to who we are at any given point in time.

The only person who has a full and complete understanding of your constellation of events is you. As you begin or continue on your journey of self-discovery and healing, just know when you interact with others, they too have had a constellation of events in their lives. This is why we need to give everyone kindness, compassion, and space, even those with whom you deeply disagree. Make room for the influences of that person's constellation of events that has shaped the person in front of you.

People who haven't had a lot of love in their life may not know how to react in a loving way until they are finally exposed to love and begin to understand what that experience is like. Some patience, space, kindness, and compassion can go a long way in our ability to interact with each other in a more harmonious way.

So I send love and compassion to you. That is, no matter what the story of my experiences has brought up for you or how it's affected you, I hope that you're sending compassion to yourself.

Chapter 6
Family Done Differently

One summer when I was around age 14, I was fortunate to start babysitting two young boys during the day. The parents owned their own business and wanted someone to be with their sons while they were at work. It was a fabulous opportunity for me. I was able to get out of my house and make some money to have a bit of independence. It also afforded me the chance to be in a different family environment and see how another family functioned.

I always wanted to experience something different than the life I had with my family. By that I mean not being surrounded by poverty, substance abuse, physical abuse, and constant chaos. I just wanted to know something different. How different? Well, two big pluses were that this family had a swimming pool, and the boys were a delight to be with. I loved being around children, especially young ones. And this family was super nice. They laughed with each other, often kissed, and they spoke to each other with respect and affection.

That normalcy was like a wonderland for me. The way this family interacted was so radically different than my family. So, the opportunity to spend 10 hours a day at their house watching their kids was… like a dream come true. Hallelujah. I knew it was good for me to spend time away from my family and experience this other world. It may sound strange, but it was such a treat to go into someone else's house and look around at pictures on the wall. I liked to see other families interact with one another, play games, or have a movie night. I was learning how I wanted my life to look, someday.

After a string of chaotic events, including my mother getting evicted, losing her job, and having her boyfriend run off, she decided to move us back to Arizona. It was the summer I turned 16. We were only in Tucson for a short time before she decided to move back to California to pursue a new relationship. I ended up traveling to California before she did so I could start the school year on time. I'd be a sophomore that fall.

I had only been in California with this man for 48 hours when he emerged from his bedroom in a pair of bikini underwear. I was lying on the couch watching TV, about to go to bed when he walked in the living room. Before I knew what was happening, he was on top of me telling me it was time for me to show him some appreciation. I was able to struggle away from him and I locked myself in the bathroom.

Before he finally passed out from drinking the entire night, he begged me to come out of the bathroom. That also was when he admitted that part of his allowing my mother to come and live there, was the possibility of having a sexual relationship with me, which my mother no doubt promised him. This wasn't a new idea for my mother. She often repeated the threat that I'd need to please her friends because she wasn't to be bothered with those activities. I was disgusted and horrified! I stayed awake all night to make sure there were no more surprises. In the morning, I dressed and left as if I were going to school. I hid at a spot around the block and waited for him to leave for work. Then I went back to pack my belongings and called a friend to come rescue me.

I relayed to my mother what had happened with her boyfriend. I told her I had no intention of ever going back to that house. Her comment was, "If you started him up, you should have finished him off. If you've ruined this relationship for me, I will never forgive you!"

Feeling shaken and not knowing where to turn, I reached out to the family I had been working for as a nanny to ask for help. They were well aware of the abuse happening in my house. I had shown up for work on a number of occasions with black eyes, swollen lips, and other bruises and wounds. They had asked me before if there was anything they could do, but there wasn't. Just allowing me to continue working for them had been an amazing blessing in my life. Now they were offering me a safe place to live. It was beyond my wildest dreams to be invited to join their family.

My mother was still in Arizona. She wouldn't make the effort to have me returned to her because I told her I'd run away no matter where I had to go. I'd stay away until I was 18 when she no longer had any legal rights with me.

After I moved in with that family, I found it was an incredible experience to live, not just work, in a completely different environment than the one I had grown up in. In some ways, it exceeded my dreams. For example, I was even invited to go on vacations with them and interact in ways I never could with my family. I'll always be deeply grateful to that family for opening their home and their hearts to me. They gave me a safe place to live and a chance to build a life that didn't include my mother. My safety was my priority because I wasn't safe with my own family. I didn't want to participate in their lifestyle.

Life with this family provided a start pointing to guide me in a new, better direction. What might be considered a simple act of kindness by them was in reality an invitation to a very troubled teenager to be part of their family. Now that I look back on it, this couldn't have been an easy decision for them. I don't know if they ever fully appreciated how their decision fundamentally changed the direction of my life.

I must admit that I didn't always make great decisions once I began living with them. Not by a long shot. And I continued to suffer the impacts of the abuse, behavior patterns, and beliefs from my past trauma. Those terrible things that I endured, still haunted me in terms of how I interacted with people, my relationships, and my lack of trust in others. Just living with that family didn't wipe out all of that. However, they did save me by providing a safe place and a stable life. If not for them, I would have lived anywhere, in a car or in other people's houses on their sofas to remain independent when I was 16. I wouldn't have gone back to live with my mother.

This was such a pivotal transitional time for me. I was able to get my GED and get my first real job. I started to put the blocks together for a good and different life from what had been modeled for me by my family.

In this safe space, I became free to think about my future. I wanted to have a husband, children, and a loving, healthy family. I thought of the birthdays, first memories, and holiday traditions that families celebrate. Holidays and traditions like Thanksgiving and Christmas were always important to me. They weren't foreign to me because I saw what they could be like when I watched movies and how friends celebrated together and bonded.

I wanted to create in my adulthood the childhood family experience that I didn't have. I always fantasized about that life when I was growing up in a house where clearly it didn't happen. In the life I imagined, we wouldn't abuse one another or beat each other. Having endured that, I always felt that the opposite experience was robbed from me, so that made me wish for it even more. I'd do anything to create a different kind of world for my husband, my children, and for myself than my world I experienced as a child.

Chapter 7
The "T" Word

Throughout my self-discovery and healing journey, one of the things I've become intimately familiar with is trauma. I've experienced varying degrees of trauma. Although, I'm not sure if I'd make the distinction among different types of trauma from my own lens. For me, trauma is trauma. However, the degree of trauma I've experienced certainly is where there were different outcomes.

More severe types of traumas are those that happen to you in the moment, such as a violent encounter, natural disaster, or car accident. It's something that happens very quickly. These are traumatic in varying degrees, depending on how you're affected by the experiences.

There's also a lower, seemingly innocuous kind of trauma, that's very subtle or an in-the-moment experience that doesn't seem traumatic at all. But sometime later, it becomes traumatic. I call this type a slow burn type of trauma. It's something that doesn't necessarily feel terribly upending in the moment, but over time it becomes an issue.

My experience with this type of trauma was when I was around nine or ten years old. My mother, brother, sister, and I were driving somewhere. I don't recall where. I remember at some point in our conversation, out of nowhere, my mother said to me, "Well, your brother and sister are actually your half brother and sister. You have a different father." That distinction about our relation didn't make sense to me at the time. I wondered what it meant. I do remember asking some questions. Unfortunately, I was just too young to understand the profound implications of that statement.

This is why I refer to that particular incident as a slow burn trauma. In the moment, it certainly made me question what it meant. But it wasn't something I ruminated on. I didn't ask a lot of questions when she first said it or in the weeks later. Asking a lot of questions about anything wouldn't have been welcomed in my household anyway. If there were an answer to be given, it'd be given the first time the question was asked. And if the answer wasn't going to be given, I could ask a million times and still not get an answer. In fact, I'd probably get an ass kicking, which would prevent me from continuing to ask the same question.

This seemingly benign comment about my half brother and sister became incredibly traumatic for me as the years went by. I realized I'd never know half of my lineage. I'd never even know my father's name! There was no way to search for him online or elsewhere to learn something about him. Even if he didn't want to have anything to do with me, at least I could understand who he was.

As a middle-aged adult, it's incredibly traumatic for me to have no way to understand half of who I am. I don't know if he had other children. There's an entire circle of relatives such as grandparents and possibly aunts, uncles, and cousins I've missed knowing. Potentially I could have had a completely different life connected to him, perhaps one that wasn't surrounded by drug addicts, alcoholics, and violent people who had no conscience and no boundaries about their behavior.

This story from my life is just a single example why it's incredibly important to understand trauma and how it can affect one's life. It can affect our body, brain chemistry, and especially thoughts. In my case, having lived in a very traumatic, chaotic situation with my immediate family for the first 16 years of my life, there was no downtime to process life-changing information.

Many of us have experienced a constant, broader level of trauma to varying degrees on a daily basis. Perhaps we were shouted at, beaten, or put in isolation. Maybe we weren't allowed any breaks to process what was going on or to recover from it.

The reason why I believe it's incredibly important to understand trauma and the impact it has on your life is because of the way that trauma manifests in your body, behavior patterns, and health. An overactive nervous system from early age trauma can result in high blood pressure, heart disease, obesity, and various stressors on the body. If the nervous system is maladjusted for a long period, its entire foundation is set in chaos.

I'm not a physician, mental health professional, or doctor of any type. I'm simply speaking from my personal experience with trauma as someone who has lived with an overactive nervous system my entire life. I've also devoted a considerable amount of time learning about trauma from a physical and psychological perspective. My goal is to share the research I've done on how to dial back the damage that's caused by trauma.

While I can't diagnose anyone's health issues or suggest medical treatments, I can recommend two books that I've found to be very informative and useful to establish a foundational understanding of trauma. Once is titled, *The Body Keeps the Score: Brain, Mind, and Body in the Healing of Trauma* by Bessel van der Kolk, M.D. I remember when I read this book it was very enlightening for me. I could start to relate differently to events, specifically how my behavior patterns and ways my body respond to what happens in my life.

The second book is, *Waking The Tiger, Healing Trauma* by Peter A. Levine. This is another book that discusses the manifestation of trauma in the human body and how that energy is stored until it is intentionally released.

One very basic way to understand the impact of having an overactive nervous system is that it destroys your circadian rhythms. It can throw off your cortisol levels—a hormone that regulates our stress response—and many other chemicals in your body. Cortisol is important because it's involved in your sleep-wake cycle and energy axis. Thus, when your nervous system is out of alignment by being overburdened for a long period of time or temporarily, the effects are body-wide and mind-wide. Symptoms show up everywhere.

Dr. van der Kolk's book discusses physical pain that can be experienced when working through trauma. I definitely can say that I've experienced that firsthand. I've felt specific pains in my body as I've worked on a traumatic situation that happened in my childhood. The pains occur as I'm resolving those particular emotions and energies. I can feel pain move through specific parts of my body because that's where that trauma has lodged itself.

Interestingly, our body lets us know where trauma is in a variety of ways. This is why I don't talk about different types of trauma. I focus on different degrees of trauma. The conversation with my mother in the car, as I described previously, was one degree of trauma. It was weird and a little bit off-putting. But that trauma by degree was completely different from the trauma I experienced at age 16 when I was raped in a park by a person who went to my school.

A group of us were in a park one night, hanging out together, playing beer drinking games. This was a core group of people that I'd known for about four years at school. I hung out with these kids daily, in class as well as after school and weekends. They were friends, not just acquaintances or classmates. At one point I left the group to use the restroom. Moments later one of the guys excused himself to use the restroom as well. He then found me, pinned me down, and raped me.

By degree that trauma was very different from any other I'd ever experienced. I felt absolute terror and horror that I was being raped. He was much stronger than I, so I couldn't defend myself. It was pitch black outside. He held his hand over my mouth as he pinned me to the ground. I couldn't scream for help. I couldn't get away. No one came to help me, but even if someone had been nearby, no one couldn't hear or see me. I was completely helpless and at the mercy of this monster whom I had gone to school with.

Due to the degree of this trauma, it took me almost a week to even remember parts of what happened. Flashes of it came in my dreams and during different activities. It took years for the full memory of that enormously traumatic experience to resurface.

It's interesting that learning about my father and being raped had a similar life changing effect on me. I knew I'd be fatherless for the rest of my life because my mother refused to tell me who my father was before she died. Plus, I had that classmate who decided to violate me at the park. That particular trauma destroyed my trust in men and in platonic male-female friendships. After that, wherever I went I always had to have an exit strategy. I'd turn down invitations to some events because there could be the possibility of encountering a dangerous situation when I couldn't protect myself. This made my world smaller, just like not knowing my father and everything that goes with such knowledge.

I believe this illustrates how it can be said that trauma is trauma in many cases, because it eventually leads back to how it created some sort of pattern or belief. It also can cause damage to our body, mind, and soul, as well as our ability to live and thrive. Maybe the distinction of the degrees of trauma can be more relevant in certain cases than others. It's those little things that happen and we just look away. We don't really think about them in a way that foretells how they're going to influence us later.

Whether it's a passing trauma or one of a high degree that rocks a person to the core, I believe it should be investigated and resolved. Just like an injury, the damaged parts need to be held, comforted, and nurtured. Those wounds should be allowed to heal so the person who has been traumatized can live life fully. Otherwise fear and limitations will be injected into the person's daily life, allowing the trauma to force the individual into a smaller and more narrow existence.

It's important to not only understand the trauma you've experienced, but also to be your own advocate to do whatever is necessary to be well, healthy, and thriving. To thrive, one doesn't have to work in a high paying job. Some lucrative salaries require long hours away from your family and enduring a miserable work environment. It's not sustainable if you come home, you're left with no energy or companionship. No matter what your work-life situation is, you must be your own fierce advocate, as your mental health, physical health, and spiritual health is at stake.

Because many aspects of our lives are intertwined, to live our best lives and thrive we must work through the traumatic experiences in our life. That includes the slow burn, seemingly innocuous events that happened at some point but later became extremely influential forces in our life. This also applies to the higher degree traumas that we're fully aware of and knocked us flat. Whether it's a calamitous situation or a slow burn event, we're never the same afterward.

I encourage you to start your effort to address your trauma with whatever tools help you. It could be to read a book about dealing with trauma, such as *The Body Keeps the Score* or it may be a different type of tool. Any tools that resonate with you will help you gain an understanding about trauma, how it affects your life, your body, your relationships, and your behavior patterns. This includes your foundational ability to feel safe, have fun, and enjoy your life.

I know how much it can help to better understand trauma because of the work I've done in my own life to resolve, nurture, and give compassion to the parts of me that held on to trauma. We can all change our lives to heal those inner wounds, those patterns. We can learn to regulate our nervous system and take care of what some people refer to as "the entire organism that we are." This includes the body, mind, and soul.

In my experience, working on trauma has been an inside job. I've had to focus on the situations that created my trauma and work through them. It has been necessary for me to work through the patterns and release those beliefs and fears related to the traumas so my life could begin to expand and open up. I admit that the inside work can be very lonely and isolating. Not everyone around me could appreciate, understand, or even want to participate in my desire to dive within and start healing the wounds so I could live a more peaceful, happy, joyful life. Many people walked away from me because of the journey I was pursuing or how I was pursuing it.

These people's actions were traumatic for me as well. I had to be at peace with releasing those people and releasing the patterns, situations, and ideas I'd lived with for so long. It was necessary for me to find the kind of life that I wanted to live. I can't say that any of this has been easy. But I can say it was easier than continuing what came before. That was when I didn't even remember the sound of my own laughter. I believe that in comparison to losing myself, my sense of humor or my joy, the journey has been well worth it. An additional benefit was my newfound ability to go to bed at night and sleep six uninterrupted hours. When I wake up in the morning, I have energy, a smile on my face, and a calm mind.

This was a complete journey of self-discovery while facing my traumas head on. There was tremendous healing from my experiences at the various stages of my journey. But for anyone, it's as simple or complex as it must be to reclaim your own life, identity, peace, and even sleep. It has been worth every moment of my investigation to get to where I am now. Now, I ask the questions: How do I make my life even better? How do I continue to heal one part of me so other parts can heal? And what wisdom will I gain from this experience?

My experience learning I had a different father than my siblings and being raped both provided me with wisdom, despite the trauma. When I detached myself from the pain and horror of those situations, it allowed me to acknowledge that wisdom. It also allowed me to heal inside. My heart is more open and lets me trust others again.

Without trust, you can't have strong, healthy relationships or friendships. Trust is the foundation that can endure the ups and downs of life, even the arguments and differences of opinion. For example, if I didn't have trust in my relationship, I'd be insecure and in a panic every time my husband and I had a difference of opinion. I might think, "Oh, my God, is he going to leave me? Is it all over?" That was a very familiar inner dialogue for me for many years. I lived in fear of losing a person I loved. The good news is that I trust my husband completely and he trusts me. I've learned that we can have differences of opinion and can compromise.

That feeling of trust is what wins the day. It won't exist if a person is riddled with insecurities and fears. If you're fearful of people who come into your life because you think they're going to hurt you, it's impossible to get to a place of trust. You won't feel safe or feel as if they are on your side. You won't be able to live a joyful, fulfilling life.

The wisdom from your past gives you the discernment to understand intuitively and more concretely which individuals are safe to trust or at least safe to take that first step with. If you feel that trust isn't likely, you don't have to dislike or disparage those people. It's just your intuition or possibly something more concrete that's telling you this isn't a relationship you should explore. Move on. That's part of what this constellation of trust gives you. It's the discernment to be able to identify experiences, situations, and relationships that are good for you or not. We always hope we know the right and wrong choices quickly so there's not much trauma associated with creating appropriate, healthy boundaries.

My message here is that exploring trauma is a critical piece of a healing journey or a journey of self-discovery. You could look at it either way. You may be someone who fully understands that you've lived a very traumatic life. Yet, you may be the type of person who says that nothing really bad ever happened to you. Know that sometimes certain memories surface for a reason. It's possible that those experiences hurt or wounded or changed you more than you fully understand and your life has been layered with un-acknowledged trauma. After all, everyone encounters some trauma in life. Take the COVID 19 for instance. It was traumatic for the entire globe in varying degrees, but everyone experienced it in some way. Therefore, we all have a collective trauma as it relates to COVID 19 and how that affected the world. We may not even be aware of how deeply it affected us personally.

Whether it's obvious or somewhat subtle, I encourage you to take the time to understand the minor and major traumas you've experienced as you embark on your journey of self-discovery and healing. There are complexities and nuances with trauma and how you could be experiencing the manifestations of those traumas. By manifestations, I mean characteristics like lower trust, varied boundaries, or insecurities. Realize that they can be somewhat subtle in your life and not feel like something you necessarily need to be concerned about.

Understand that I say this not to frighten you or to say, "Oh my God, you know, if I hadn't had trauma, I'd be a perfect person," because that situation doesn't exist. This is once again my intention to encourage you to be your own advocate. Learn about the things that have influenced your life, shaped your belief patterns, and built your habit patterns. It's ideal if you can operate from a place of authenticity—a state of being that hasn't been shaped, shifted, reduced, or limited by your experiences in life. Your goal is to live, thrive, and enjoy your life even though this world isn't always peaceful and thriving. If we're peaceful and thriving as individuals, then we have the ability to experience life differently and to potentially help others experience their lives differently.

This is an inside job. You must go and find the things, the breadcrumbs within and bring compassion to them. Bring light, nurturing, safety, and healing to them. Most importantly, bring love to them. Strive to bring love to the situations that were harmful, chaotic, and traumatic, even those that in the moment seemed as though you were never going to survive them. By doing so you can begin to resolve whatever pain might still be attached to them. Gain wisdom and learn from all your experiences. Also have some additional space and freedom within your heart and life to expand your own experience to live, thrive, and love your every day.

It's certain that we'll continue to have ups and downs through life. We'll continue to learn about ourselves along the way. There's no such thing as being able to say, "Oh, I'm done. I don't need to think about this anymore. I'm just going to move on with my life." That's because life is an endless learning process. By acknowledging this, you can learn to be authentic. You also can continue to bring compassion and healing to yourself, so you'll have the ability to show up for others, help them, and influence situations in positive ways. You can only do this if you have a peaceful, nurturing, learning process operating inside. Yes, it's absolutely an inside job.

Chapter 8
Secure Your Mask First

As you read this book and learn about the details of my experiences, it may bring up some memories of life events that have happened to you. These may include things that friends have told you or you've read about over the years.

It's my hope that you become more curious about those memories and how your experiences have affected you. Maybe you're questioning why certain memories are coming to mind while you read. The reason I mention this is because we all reach a point where we require something to change in our lives, a different way must be found.

I call my pivotal point my red light moment, sitting in my car at that stoplight. Your moment may have taken place or will occur in any number of different situations. Our lives are unique, with histories and experiences that have affected us in positive and challenging ways. At some point, they come together at a decision point unlike anyone else's.

Our memories that have shaped us in so many ways can involve different types of traumas. Experiencing trauma as a child doesn't require having been abused by a caretaker or someone in your home. It could've been the trauma that you encountered from having a car or bicycle accident, being bullied at school, or enduring a particularly mean teacher. Whatever the trauma you experienced, you arrive at a moment when the pressure, the intensity of your response to that trauma, is so strong that something must change.

In that moment, I'd encourage you to slow down and secure your mask first. What I mean by securing your mask first is the need to make your wellbeing your first priority, as in the airline safety speech. We tend to go out of our way to help or support someone without making sure we are properly provided for, which can create more problems than solutions. If you aren't well rested, fed, and feeling grounded then you cannot truly be of service to someone else. In a way you're distracted by your own needs. This can inadvertently cause you to resent the very person you're wanting to help.

When you recognize the need for change, you may not have a partner or be moving away from your family. You might need to make many different decisions about your life, not just one or two big ones. My case is just one example, as everyone's first steps are different because each person's situation and state of mind are different. However, the critical thing is to determine what you need to change first and then get started.

As I sat in my apartment after my separation, I began to understand my pattern of seeking happiness outside myself needed to stop. I had always scoffed at the notion that you can't love someone else until you love yourself. I still question that to a degree, so I would say it differently as, "You cannot know how to love someone else until you learn how to love yourself." This is an important nuance. I have loved other people in my life and yet I am just now starting to create that relationship with myself. I would say the difference is, if you're loving other people only through the lens of them accepting you, that's not love. That's trying to belong by abandoning yourself. It may work for a while, but it's superficial and conditional.

Truly loving yourself is saying kind things to yourself when you've just made an enormous blunder. When you truly love yourself there's compassion and possibly even humor, if humor is appropriate for the situation. More often than not, our blunders are followed by a long and bloody beating delivered to ourselves from ourselves.

That was what I kept in mind as I reviewed my history of when people were good to me—kind and generous. Generally those times were when they needed or wanted something from me. At first, I was very resentful describing my friends as people who only chose to be around me when they needed something. For example, my bosses usually were good to me because I was always working harder than my colleagues. That was because I constantly felt like I needed to earn my role. I didn't have the fancy degrees. All of this made me feel like the person who was *lucky* to be in the room. It slowly dawned on me that all across my life, in all of my relationships, I was constantly asking permission to exist. I never actually felt like I belonged anywhere, so if I outperformed everyone I would have a reason to be present. If you're always trying to earn your place in the room, conversation, or event then you don't have a firm foundation within yourself. That means you'll always be at the mercy of the external situation, person, or people.

I knew I had to shift away from this external need for affirmation to own the changes I was making in my life. Think of this as a pivot away from external cues to trust internal cues. Of course, your first aha moment could be very different from that. It could involve the way you set boundaries in your relationships or the way you allow people to talk to you.

This is why I suggest that you become curious as you examine your experiences and decisions. Then ask yourself which decisions are the right ones for you to make in various situations. No two situations are the same and therefore the remedies will be different. Even the smallest nuances could be different. After all, each one of us has a different life story. All our experiences and the decisions that flow from those experiences are unique. Even more depth in this process comes from the wisdom we've collected over time, based on hearing other people's stories and their remedies.

You can use this approach and knowledge as a backdrop when you begin your journey. It helps to answer the question, "Where do I begin?" If you're feeling you need to begin slowly, perhaps start with finding a book or watching a video online rather than talking with another person or interacting with a group. Or do you need something more interactive? Could that take the form of a sounding board? Would it be more appropriate to engage a therapist, coach, or a close trusted friend for your situation? Perhaps you want to learn within in a group experience. That could allow you to participate in a desired activity as a member of a community.

Understand that each of us will approach this moment of change differently because the experiences that got us to a key moment of realization are unique. Therefore, the remedy and how we pursue it will be different for each of us. I want to be very clear that there's no right or wrong way to do this. I will say that the more you take ownership of your desire to change and where you want to begin, the more successful you'll be in finding tools that resonate with where you want to go on your journey. In other words, it likely would be an unsuccessful effort if you rely on external people or external sources to tell you what they think you should fix, work on, or do and how to do it.

Don't get me wrong. I'm not against people recommending coaches, therapists, books, and other resources. That's wonderful and it's often how people begin their journeys to some level of healing. I'm suggesting that even those closest to us may not totally understand the scale and complexities of what we're trying to accomplish. It's critical that you trust yourself, your "knowing," to make such important decisions.

So, the important point here is to begin with that first step. If the grand world of self-help is too big or too intimidating, consider starting small. You could do an internet search for a book about your specific trauma or experience. There are tools at your fingertips to narrow the search for how and where you want to begin your journey. It might be a good idea to look at several books to determine if what the authors are saying fits what you're looking for. Do you understand the information presented on the book jacket or introduction? Does it make sense to you? What you're looking for is resonance. What feels right to you, what reads easily, what situations do the authors address that connect with you?

For some of us, a book will lead to a life-changing experience, an aha moment. Some people may have an intuitive experience, in which they sense something or feel like instinctive forces are at work. This could be revealing an emotional or mental state. Others may have a somatic or bodily experience, meaning they get a physical feeling in their gut when they know something is right. Conversely, they get that sick feeling inside when they know something is wrong. Pay attention to the cues your mind and body provides. They are part of your experience in the sacred story you're exploring.

It's incumbent upon you to do the necessary research on books or other resources and pay attention to the experience you're having as you review these resources. Consider what's jumping out at you upon an initial look. Because the authors or creators aren't going to personally help you, their words will need to move you forward or sideways or point you in a new direction. That's why you should continue to monitor what's happening through your internal responses.

Now that I mention it, your internal responses are important aspects to keep in mind in whichever way you engage with the self-help world. That's because your sacred journey involves a search for people and resources that resonate with you and can help you along your journey. This is especially the case with books. As time goes by and you have more experiences, you might read other books by the same author. Sometimes a foreword or review by another author will move you to explore his or her books. Some books will resonate with you, while others won't. Not connecting with an author doesn't make that person or the book bad. It just means it wasn't right for you, so you just move on to the next book. We even gain knowledge from efforts that don't work even if it's only that they narrow down the options on what might work.

The world of self-help books is fabulous. There's an endless array of tools, ideas, and concepts out there. I believe everybody in the self-help world is genuinely trying to help people. They really want to put their knowledge forward, their stories out there, and their experiences in the spotlight to help others. Ultimately, their hope is to reach at least one person and prevent that person from suffering. That's the fuel that drives healers to do what they can for others. Be open-minded when you read a book that seems promising. However, manage your expectations about how much that learning experience will affect you.

This is a little point I want to make but remember that if you recommend a book to others and they don't like it, don't take it personally. Maybe that message didn't resonate with them at that time. Who knows, maybe a year from now they'll pick up the book again and it'll be the sun, the moon, and the stars at that time. Timing can be everything.

I also want to mention the resources available on internet platforms like YouTube. They have a huge library of videos by knowledgeable people, as well as individuals sharing their life experiences. Content is presented as speeches, workshops, webinars, and even conversations. They offer many methodologies and perspectives from narrow to broad topics that might touch on your area of focus. That said, be aware that the speakers' qualifications and the quality of the content they provide vary widely.

Along the same lines as general videos are TED® talks. Speakers are vetted by a review team to maintain a reasonable level of quality and credibility. Just as with books, some messages will resonate with you and others will not. But they all are guideposts you can use that result from your organic decisions and efforts, not from your enculturation or the belief patterns that no longer serve you.

An additional tool I should mention is to make audio recordings and then listen to them. This can be a powerful practice to record your thoughts with your own voice. It's an effective way to connect the tone of your voice and strength of your words with the changes you're considering. Audio journaling can be revealing, knowing where you are in your journey when you were doing that recording. It can be challenging to recognize this from written journaling alone. That's because you're only getting a one-dimensional experience from written words. Those words certainly will evoke feelings or have feelings baked in but hearing them is different. Audio recordings can provide a good feedback loop for you.

I want to pass along something I've learned, in terms of journaling and writing in general. It's a very powerful tool to sit and write down your feelings, whether this writing is private or you plan to share it. Note that sharing may be with others but there's also sharing of your thoughts with the universe. Words become even more powerful when you write them. Keep this in mind.

I've often advised clients to write about their experiences. This could be writing a letter to someone with whom they were experiencing a conflict or just daily journaling during a difficult period in their life or relationships. Once they've written the words, assuming this isn't something they're planning to share, an option is to destroy the paper. Rip it up. Burn it. Shred it. Whatever felt right. The point is do not keep the words in your space.

There is a lot of energy that goes into spilling emotions on the paper and we don't want to invite that energy to hang around. Keeping the words nearby also keeps the experience and the emotions nearby. Therefore, it may be best to release the words so our healing can begin.

For instance, in my mid-30s it was clear my mother was never going to apologize for her behavior. She was never going to acknowledge the abuse, the hateful words, or the pain I continued to feel from abandonment in my childhood. I decided it was time for me to finally have my say, so I wrote her an eight-page letter. I used that opportunity to say all the things I was never allowed to say. I brought up specific situations in which I had been deeply hurt with the pain that I never acknowledged.

I spent several days on that letter. I knew it was the only time I would take this kind of action, so I wanted to make sure I said all there was to say. Once I was satisfied, I mailed the letter. I can't say that I let it all go, but I did feel an enormous weight lifted because I finally had been able to speak my words, my truth. A reply wasn't expected, or necessary. I had finally spoken and no one could take that away from me. It supported my belief that all roads must lead back to our own peace of mind.

But suppose at this point you feel like there's more to understand than you can manage on your own. That's when you may decide to work with a professional. In the same way I recommended considering books, I suggest that you interview several professionals before you engage one. Most professionals I've crossed paths with offer an initial meeting for free. This gives you and the professional you're potentially going to work with an opportunity to talk with each other to determine if what you're working on falls within that person's area of expertise.

Based on my experience, what's even more important is determining if you have a good connection with that person. Do you feel comfortable with that individual? Do you feel like you could build trust? For this to be a successful engagement, know that you'll need to be incredibly vulnerable during the sessions. If you don't feel safe and you can't be vulnerable, chances are you won't have a successful outcome.

You want to try and avoid a situation in which the professional whom you believe is going to help you, either doesn't help or worse makes you feel like you've lost some of your prior progress. This could occur if you are unable to communicate effectively. Maybe you don't feel safe, there is no resonance between the two of you, or potentially the professional doesn't have the necessary level of expertise regarding your needs.

A common risk when walking away from an unsuccessful engagement is that you may think you did something wrong, failed, just didn't get it, or weren't smart enough to understand. There are many negative beliefs that can result from an unsuccessful engagement. Unfortunately we don't tend to point the finger at the professional, as we often assume the blame and consider ourselves failures. They are the professionals, right? They have the training and the fancy degree, so obviously they know what to do. Right? Wrong. This is no criticism of their talents, as they wouldn't be in their line of work if they weren't talented. But that doesn't mean they're the right fit for you.

For this reason, I strongly encourage you to do your homework on prospective coaches, therapists, or counselors. This is your sacred life, not theirs. And while they can hold space for you, provide direction, and make tools available, there must be a deep connection for that person to help guide you through your healing. It would be magnificent if the first person you work with could be the only person you ever need, but the prospect of one person being the entire solution is an unrealistic expectation.

If you're required to only work with one professional because of health insurance limitations, I'd suggest collaborating with the policy administrator. Do your best to explain that you need someone else to work with if that first person isn't a good fit. This is your time, your life, your money. You want to be working with a professional who's going to respect your sacred journey and be the right guide at this point in your journey. Over time as you grow, many of the resources you need will change, even where you find resonance changes. Growth, in anything, is an ever-expanding journey.

Groups and seminars or larger gatherings, such as conferences and conventions, also may play a role in your journey. This can involve group therapy, group coaching, and activities with other people who are hosted or facilitated by a professional, author, or guide.

A group I had been affiliated with for several years followed a certain spiritual organization, not a church but definitely a group with its own belief systems and teachings. During my time with this group, I was desperately seeking new friends, especially women my age. The organization they followed was doing their annual "introduction to their teachings" seminar in Denver. I didn't know much about their teachings, but I really wanted to fit into this group. This seemed like a way to do that and it could potentially be beneficial to me, so why not?

My experience was a nightmare, other than meeting a lovely woman whom I still call a friend. From the moment the seminar began I knew it was a mistake. First, their presentation style was demeaning and condescending. If you weren't already following their program then obviously you were lost and miserable. Each of the presentations were distributed, projected, and then read aloud verbatim. That particular style puts me to sleep. I'm being read to and there's no new information being presented. This is just story time!

The ego at the core of their belief system was as close to a cult as I ever want to experience. Here's what I mean. There was an exercise on the second day to be done under supervision to ensure you mastered the task. I must have mentioned to someone that my husband had read one of their books. When it was my turn to be observed by the instructor, rather than having me do the exercise she spent 20 minutes grilling me on where my husband found their book. Had he shared it? Had I read it? Who had he discussed it with? The entire confrontation was unreal.

Again, through my own desperation to belong I went to a second seminar with that same organization. This time it was held at their headquarters. Some of the folks I shared my experience with thought perhaps I had a bad team or bad teachers, but I shouldn't discount the teachings because of those people. I decided to be optimistic and my husband was coming with me so it would be a better experience. Nope. That entire organization was driven by ego and outright telling people if they don't follow them, they're lost. It felt like they were indoctrinating their new members right in front of my eyes. It was an unsettling experience.

On the flight home from the second seminar, I had to admit to myself that I had zero in common with the people in my group, apart from the ceremony space. As intense and meaningful as that space was, the pain of healing from that space along with integrating the information from my personal journey was too much to bear. I tried to be kind to myself for suffering through two of those seminars just to be accepted by the people in the group. As you know by now, this was a deeply held pattern of survival within my immediate family, to conform or feel their wrath.

However, as an adult I now have many more choices and I don't want to spend my time in any environment where I'm just trying to belong. By trying to belong, I've already abandoned myself and am no longer operating within my own integrity. I made a pact with myself on the flight home that I wouldn't put myself in that position again. I was and still am on a self-discovery journey so discovering what doesn't work is every bit as important as finding what does. As it turns out, the seminars were deeply transformative and by that definition quite successful. That said, I certainly don't suggest learning through misery if it can be avoided.

You'll always gain wisdom from everything you experience, from every encounter, book, seminar, and ways you engage. Each situation is an invitation to expand, to learn something new. Each of the coaching engagements I've experienced have had drawbacks. Some negative aspects were huge and others minor. Yet, I learned something important, even if it was what not to do. It's all important. It's all necessary. And it's all part of the journey.

On the other hand, a group experience can be fantastically liberating. One step I took was to go on a seven-day silent retreat at a monastery. Each day we worked together on particular topics as a group. Other than the time in our workshops, we didn't engage with each other. We weren't allowed to make eye contact and we didn't speak, even while we were eating.

As an extrovert, that amount of silence was alarming at first. It's hard to describe how loud the world is once you've experienced that interactive silence. By the third day, I could feel my body start to relax very deeply, not in a kicked-back sort of way but in an "Oh. I can stop and breathe" feeling. As a person who spent the first half of her life with one foot in poverty and the other on a banana peel, stopping and breathing had never been an option.

During the workshops, we only communicated in very defined roles. That's when we'd ask questions and have something like conversational interactions. It was fascinating for me to be in a situation where the one primary strength I had leaned on, speech, was unavailable to me. I'm of course used to the notion of being seen and not heard, but this was a very different environment. The required silence and lack of eye contact were symbols of deep respect for each individual. For the first time, I couldn't use speech to influence or impact anything. Because of this restriction, I wasn't getting to know the other people or making friends or connections.

When I was at the monastery out in the wilderness, I took daily walks and reflected on the material we were learning. I believe I had one of my biggest epiphanies at the monastery primarily because speaking was taken away from me. Without the ability to connect with the other members of the group, I couldn't use their signals to determine if I was fitting in or if I needed to adjust something. I only had my own thoughts about what was happening. My epiphany occurred during a walk one afternoon before dinner. When I stopped to stare out across the horizon in the hilly, tree covered country, I realized it was quiet. Not only quiet outside, but it was quiet inside my mind and body. I don't think I'd ever realized just how much noise went on in my head all the time before that moment.

In that quiet, I realized how much of my life I'd given away to all the external authorities, meaning everybody including my caregivers, friends, boyfriends, husbands, and bosses. If they said I was okay, then I was okay. But if they said I wasn't okay, then I definitely was not okay. I stood on that hill like I was watching a movie about how I'd taken my cue from others as to whether or not I was okay.

It was in that quiet space, without all the noise and chaos in my head, I thought, "Wow, I can actually be okay all by myself with no one else's help or opinions." I had moments of independence, joy, and things like that before, but this was different. This was me taking back my opinion of myself and starting to create a new opinion of myself from the internal authority. It was from my own sacred self.

During that week-long group program, I was totally out of my comfort zone. Part of that was because I was silent, without interpersonal interactions going on. Still, the people, the subject, and the environment resonated with me. You don't have to be in your comfort zone to be in the right place. I was totally out of my comfort zone there, but I was absolutely in the right place.

Taking all this into account, I want to make the point that you can choose one or all of the paths you come across. Before you engage with any of them, be sure to listen to yourself first. And make sure that each experience you choose to have is the right one for you. It's one that you're choosing for yourself. Other people may have recommended it, but you're the one who's determining if it's a good fit for you.

You're deciding for yourself that you want to take the next step, whatever that is. Then you take that step and the next step. At times, some of those steps may feel like you're taking ten steps backward. That can be very deflating. But this journey is not linear. There's no natural middle or end even if there's a natural beginning. Then again, there might be more than one beginning. Don't allow the windy road to intimidate you, because all journeys have their course changes along the way. This is a marathon, not a sprint. Patience is the key.

One additional concept I've become comfortable with is that there's no end, no finish line to our journeys. I believe once you start, you never stop. There's never going to be a single book, person, or weekend retreat anywhere that's going to solve all the mysteries, issues, problems, or concerns that you're dealing with. There always will be more to explore. There are thousands of elements connected to your journey after the moment you realize change is required.

Remember to continuously check in with yourself and make sure you're in the right place with the right materials and the right people. If you're not, change what needs to be changed. Then, carry on and stay curious.

Chapter 9
Dancing in the Dining Room

Although I wanted to build a new life with a totally different kind of partner than the ones I'd seen with my mother, my underlying habits and behaviors continued. I found myself in relationships in which those negative types of patterns continued to surface. It took me until I was 46 and divorced three times to understand that I continually attracted the same type of person. Each relationship followed the same destructive pattern.

After I left my third husband, I made a commitment to myself that I was going to do the work necessary to understand why I kept repeating the same pattern. The pattern I wanted was the one I saw in that wonderful family I lived with in California when I was 16.

One image that reflects what I wanted and deserved was of the parents who took me in. The image is of them dancing together in their dining room at night after they put the boys to bed. I might be watching TV while they were having a cocktail and dancing, all the time smiling at each other. They were always kind to each other as well as sexy and flirty with each other.

It's easy to understand why that became my model relationship. Imagine two people who can work, live, travel, play, and raise two healthy, happy children together. I'm not saying they didn't have any difficulties. They were like any other married couple who had their spats and disagreements. But fundamentally, these two people truly loved each other. When they danced in the dining room, you could tell the way they looked at each other there was profound, deep love between them.

That's why I started looking for a man who would dance with me in the dining room. And when he looked at me, I could see the love in his eyes. Fast forward to today. I've lived in this beautiful relationship for several years now and it is everything I expected, fantasized about and even more.

I was shattered in my mid-forties because of my repeated unhealthy behaviors and deep, unconscious patterns and beliefs that attracted me to my former partners. Even though I kept striving for the type of relationship my nanny family modeled for me, the relationships I actually had were much closer to the relationships modeled by my mother and stepfather.

This realization prompted me to begin unpacking all of my trauma and behavioral baggage that resulted in my repeated behavior. I began just by asking myself questions. How does this happen? How do I keep attracting the same type of person? And more importantly, how can I begin to attract something different? How can I use this experience of having lived with my model family and seeing their open exchange of love?

I remember that even if they had argued in the morning, they could be dancing in the dining room together in the evening. They might be cuddled up on the couch watching a movie together or talking while they shared a bottle of wine sitting outside with their feet in the pool. These two people who had worked together all day, still enjoyed one another's company.

Even though that couple's behavior had been modeled for me and it was what I was striving for, that's not what I found in my relationships. It was a reckoning for me to understand how I could prevent this pattern from continuing and create another, better pattern. After all, I already knew what my ideal relationship looked like. How could I recreate that in my life?

It was this quest that opened the vast universe of available self-help resources. I started to work through my behaviors, learned from various teachers, read more books, and attended multiple seminars. I began to be a better advocate for myself. For example, if I were involved in a therapy program, I learned to speak up and say that I appreciated what the program offered or what it didn't address in relation to what I needed to work on at that time. It was empowering to feel the confidence to say something didn't align with my focus and choose to find something else that did.

One of the important messages here is that self-advocacy kept me on point in my journey. I continually asked myself, what is it that I'm working on? What am I trying to uncover? What am I thoughtfully looking at? Then, regarding my relationships, I'd look for a bridge between what I was experiencing and what I wanted.

This motivated me to start doing a lot of research about the internal dynamics of relationships. Ultimately, I found what it comes back to is the fact that our journey of self-discovery and healing is an inside job. We have to go inside to find where the triggers are, as well as the patterns and beliefs. Is it a statement someone made? Is it something we observed? Is it a memory that we had? Is it something we're projecting onto a situation that's the trigger?

If we don't remain present in a situation, we can't begin the process of understanding the links between our behaviors and relationships. We must be present as well as very aware and focused on what we're trying to work on. Once we do that, it's about finding the resources that align with what our needs are.

Consider it this way. You're not going to visit an eye doctor and expect a prescription for your hearing. You'd go to an audiologist for a hearing appointment. In that same way, you want to make sure that whatever it is you're doing, reading, or attending aligns with your focus at that time. Have a plan if you have an ongoing relationship with a mental health professional, coach, therapist, or psychiatrist. And if that person you're working with isn't helping you focus on the right things, speak up. Change the relationship or switch to a different person.

Again, two of the most important lessons to learn is that you must be your own advocate and you have to work on what's present for you. Only you know what that is.

A takeaway from my previous marriage that led to my red light moment was that I needed to work on how to operate in relationships. If I kept operating in ways that were the opposite of where my happiness was, I'd simply keep repeating what resulted in unhappiness. I needed to start operating in ways that were aligned with my happiness and to advocate for this. It was my responsibility to find the resources to help me with that specific situation and specific set of circumstances. My intuition told me that the first steps would be like setting a row of dominoes in motion.

Once you start feeling more comfortable about attracting the right kind of person or putting up the right boundaries, you don't attract the same kind of person as before. The next dominos fall. Those actions open up other lines of inquiry about how you are in relationships, where you find your relationships, how serious you are, and what kind of relationships you're even looking for. These pieces start falling into place.

For much of my life, I was very specific about wanting to get married and I only wanted to be married once. Divorce was out of the question. It was very important to me to have everything in a relationship that I think most people genuinely hope for at the outset of stepping into married life. For me, this also included having children. Yet, if I were going to have children, I needed to trust my partner to be a good, loving father to these children, even if our relationship crumbled. That level of trust was extremely important to me, so I was very present to that.

This is a perfect illustration for how important it is that you become very present for the things that are most important to you, especially with relationships. Then you look at your life and see how aligned it is with those foundational aspects built from the inside out. Only you can look at your life through the filters of what's present and what's important to you. Only you can determine what's there and where you are on your journey.

In the context of my story about the family that took me in plus my troubled relationships, I still believed in marriage even after my third marriage. I still believed in having a relationship in which I could dance with my husband in the dining room, have fun together, and love each other passionately even when we disagree with each other or face challenges.

I still believed that was possible and I wanted it in my life. Almost 10 years later upon my eighth anniversary with my husband, I've never been so in love in my life. I've never felt as seen and heard as I do in this relationship. There's safety for us to disagree with each other and forgive each other. And yes, there is dancing in the dining room as we gaze at each other with deep, passionate love.

I can see a future with him. I can see growing old with him. This is because I'm finally in a relationship that was modeled for me by that family I nannied for. Furthermore, I did the work on myself to figure out how I could show up and be a real partner with my husband.

How do you find and embrace the type of partner who will dance with you in the dining room? The process doesn't need to feel like a burden. It can be a beautiful, magical unfolding of who you are so you're in a place where those magical things can happen. The overarching theme behind this part of your journey is moving forward with love, gratitude, and openness. And don't forget to stay curious!

The inside out with relationships

When it comes to relationships I like to say, the more you heal the better you feel. The more you can see, the more you can take in, and the more life has to offer. I urge you not to be intimidated by the concept of this being an *inside job*. Be empowered by that because it means you're in control to drive yourself to the place where you're going to feel happy and at peace. No one else can do it for you. You have the opportunity to do this for yourself and enjoy all that you discover along your self-discovery journey.

I don't refer to this "place" where I am as an end state because I don't feel like I'm at an end state in my life. Even though I'm celebrating this wonderfully happy relationship I now enjoy, I have plenty of other things that I'm still working on. The happiness in my marriage gives me the space, the safety, and the encouragement to explore and reach for new things. I believe I'm in a state of being where I can continue learning about myself. I find special joy knowing that my husband completely supports my journey and I completely support his self-knowledge journey too.

It's amazing to know the relationship I saw in that dining room when I was 16 actually is possible for me. I'm finally living it. The reason is because I embraced and celebrated the fact that it was an inside job. I no longer needed to believe that someone else was going to fix me. I was going to be the one doing the work.

When you realize your healing is in your own hands, that's a fabulously empowering moment. You understand that you don't need to rely on anything or anybody else. You're going to finally step into doing this for yourself.

I'm now doing all I can so I can live and thrive in my relationships. In doing so, the people around me also will benefit because our relationships are affected by my changes. All of this comes from that wonderful life-fulfilling circle of goodness in which I'm in a constant state of learning, growing, evolving with gratitude, living with empowerment, and knowing.

I own this, from the inside out. Hallelujah. I'm strong enough to deflect what others might tell me to do, to wear, to look like, and that other garbage. At the end of the day, each of us is the architect of our entire world. Wow. What can we make with that?

Chapter 10
Beyond Childhood Trauma

As you'd expect, I acknowledge many lessons learned from my childhood experiences. An important one is that it's not right to make an enemy of your past, your behavior patterns, or your belief patterns.

Our task is to understand our past and acknowledge the origins of things that no longer resonate with us so we can create things that do resonate. We can accomplish this by interacting with our environment and world in ways that are more resonant with us and our nature. This is instead of interacting due to imposed belief systems and patterns from our childhood, peers, work, and colleagues. We know that belief systems come from everywhere. It's particularly true in the digital age in which there's information about everything invading our awareness all the time at levels that can be overwhelming. This can stir up and compound experiences, especially those from childhood.

Underneath my terrible, chaotic experience as a youth has been a deep love and respect for that little girl who handled herself amazingly, bravely, and courageously in such terrifying moments. It's not about making any part of her bad. It's about bringing her whole self into the present and removing the layers of conditioning and cultural indoctrination. These are the layers of culture and society that tell us what we're supposed to do, when, how, and with whom.

Removing all that allows us just to be ourselves. It gives us much more space and dimension to work with in terms of where we go from the place we are. We're freed up from the past to ask, "What do I choose to do with my time? What people do I choose to spend my time with? What do I choose to take in as entertainment, information, or news?"

When we operate from a place of choice about what we want to bring into our life, we're functioning at a much higher and more energetic vibration. By the word vibration I mean the energy or energetic resonance we feel sometimes. This signals that our sense of peace is at hand and that it's part of our story—the story of hope and about finding that place of peace. As that little girl found her place, the grown woman she became found her place.

I believe you can find your own place of peace. Some call this sovereignty. It's about engaging in a journey of curiosity, hope, empathy, courage, and compassion. This process can help you remove the trauma from your body, from your mind, and from your life. It also helps your nervous system operate from a place of calm—a compatible, energetic vibration or resonance—so your body and mind can work effectively. That's even though it never will attain such a state every hour nor every day. The key is to work with the situations in your life and move toward establishing a sense of peace and balance as part of your new habitual patterns.

Chapter 11
Burn the Boats

A year or two into my self-discovery and healing journey. I met a couple of people with whom I could be completely honest about my story, my healing, and what I was trying to accomplish in terms of feeling better about myself and belonging. At one point, a friend of mine sat me down to discuss a therapeutic approach.

I learned that a group—a community—gathered quarterly and used plant-based medicine journeys together as part of their therapeutic process. Now as you may imagine, this approach brought up many issues due to my having grown up with substance abuse at home. The whole concept of using any substance was absolutely out of the question for me. Part of my vow to myself was to be different from my family. That had everything to do with not engaging in substance use or abuse.

This issue and my commitment even came up in my work life. Every once in a while, I'd sit at the lunch table at work and someone would start talking about smoking pot. Everyone around the table would share their experiences. They'd look at me and not a single person at that table believed me when I said I'd never tried it. I always said the same thing, to be honest. I imagine they all just thought I didn't want to confess.

So, the concept of what my friend was presenting with the use of medicines, even for therapeutic purposes, was horrifying to me. My internal response was... no. I mean an absolute no with an exclamation mark. Picture all the mental and emotional gates closing and locks locking in my head.

My friend looked at me and said, "Come on. You know me. You know that's not who I am." I sat judgmentally, but quietly. I asked what they did during these gatherings. My friend explained, "Please listen to the end with an open mind." I said I would. Keep in mind that this was a person I had a lot of respect for. The revelation about this medicinal approach was stunning, nonetheless. I convinced myself to set aside my judgments, prejudices, and past experiences to listen to what my friend had to say.

A caveat here is that during my prior marriage, my husband used cannabis for his pain from some severe sports injuries. Rather than take prescription painkillers, he used cannabis. When this was introduced in our relationship before we were married, it triggered memories and traumatized me due to the association with my family. I was about to break up with him when he asked me to do him the favor of conducting some research on cannabis use for medicinal purposes. Coincidentally at the time, I was pursuing a degree program and needed to write a research paper. So, I decided to write a paper on cannabis to do what he asked and satisfy my educational requirement.

I found through my research that his beliefs about using cannabis were true. Because I lived with him, I knew he wasn't an abuser. My research and writing the paper on cannabis helped start cracking open many of those beliefs for me. Prior to that, drugs were the devil, period, end of sentence. But researching and writing that paper helped open my own mind. I better understood what was actually happening in society with cannabis with all the medical patient use.

Having done this research and seen my husband's experience made me be more open-minded in the conversation with my friend about the group's treatment approach. The members of this group all knew each other quite well. They had a weekend-long ceremony revolving around a specific issue they were struggling with or were curious about. They all shared how they were doing, what was on their minds, and what was present for them. My friend also described the types of themes that people were working on, without compromising anyone's confidentiality. And everyone went to bed alone. This was all very on the straight and narrow.

I asked my friend why the group would share this experience with me. Why were they inviting me to it? I learned that it was due to the scope of abuse I had suffered and the depth of the trauma I'd been through. They knew it would take forever to address all this in once-a-week therapy sessions. Since my friend had been involved with this group for some time, their track record was impressive in that people had shed years of trauma as quickly as in eight hours of the experience. It was quite a relief for people to be able to move through that amount of trauma and rid it from their space, their minds and bodies. I sat there quietly because what my friend said made a lot of sense and resonated with me.

They told me the first morning of the program that all the participants would use a substance, a medicine. Then, we'd lie down on a mat for the day with an eyeshade and headphones on. Each of us would have a unique personal experience. I'm certain there was a collective energy created because these people were releasing and growing and shedding emotion-packed experiences.

Later in the evening, the participants would eat some light food. Then they'd share what was happening in their lives, drink lots of water to stay hydrated and write in their journals. Everyone would go to bed after that.

The next morning, they got up and had a big breakfast. Afterward, they came together to share their thoughts prompted by questions such as: "How are you doing?" and "What was your experience?" Both individual experiences and collective experiences were shared.

All of this—the personal and group experiences—was really hard for me to process because I thought I couldn't participate in a process based on medicines. I'd be the biggest hypocrite if I used chemical substances. I've vilified my family for all their substance abuse and separated from them irreversibly because of it. I couldn't go and participate in that type of activity now. Wouldn't that make me like them? Would I have to let them back into my life if I do this?

It was as if an emotional volcano went off inside of me. And it was a fight that started between how much sense my friend made and how these thoughts of hypocrisy felt. In addition to this, I experienced fear. Frankly, because of the things I had seen my family do under the influence of narcotics and alcohol, this approach terrified me. It disgusted me, to be honest. I wanted nothing to do with anything of that nature. I'm sure my friend could read all of this as I sat there silently, just processing the information.

"Sorry," my friend said. "I know how conflicted you are about this because of your mom and your past. But I'd encourage you to think about it this way, Tawnya. Your family used substances criminally and abusively. Here, you'll be partnering with medicines to heal those deep wounds you carry from the child abuse, abandonment, neglect, rejection, and from the daily terror that was present for many years."

My daily terror was from asking, "Is today going to be the day I die?" Imagine what that does to your body, your mind, and your spirit.

I turned to the deep respect I had for this friend. Then, I asked how I could engage with this group. My friend explained that I would meet with the facilitator to be evaluated. If this worked for me, I'd feel safe in knowing this was a path that I wanted to embark on. After all, this medicine path was one of those actions that once you engage in you can't put that genie back in a bottle.

I say "burn the boats"—and use that as this chapter's title—because you're never the same person after a psychedelic experience. That's whether you remember the experience or not, as you're deeply transformed in any case. In part, this contributes to the boundlessness of the self-discovery journey. Once you encounter the enormity of everything and nothing, your curiosity is never again fully quenched. There's always another mystery to be solved.

Please understand that I'm not offering this or other approaches as recommendations or advocacy for the medicine path. I only tell you this based on my set of experiences and lessons learned along my journey.

Understand that I made the decision to take that first step with this group because doctors, psychologists, and coaches weren't helping me. I was navigating my healing with books. Some were the most effective up to that point because I was digesting them through my own filters and lenses. Reading helped me find at least some of the information I was seeking. But I realized books didn't completely fill the void.

When I met with the group's facilitator, we discussed all the rules. It was critical for me to learn about the facilitator's experience, as well as this professional's depth and breadth of experience with cases like mine. I also wanted to understand what all this meant in terms of my health and safety. After much deliberation and internal consideration, I decided to move forward.

Before I joined the group, I told no one in my life about it. The only one who knew was the friend who referred me to the group. This was very personal and private to me. It was an extremely complicated and hard decision for me to make.

As I weighed how I wanted to feel and improve my health, my intuition told me this was the right thing to do. I trusted my own counsel and my research, along with my desire to heal. I didn't expect to be an entirely different person overnight. It's difficult to say what my expectations were going in, but I believe I was anticipating that this path would help expedite my healing. Maybe it would help me see and feel the changes and the gains in my day-to-day life, in my experience of living.

I participated with this group for about four years. Nearly all my experiences ended up being productive. Even so, many experiences I had were a mixed bag of positive and negative, emotionally and physically. The main issue was that I never felt like I was part of the group—on an equal standing or accepted as a valued participant. When a situation like this occurs, especially when we're in a vulnerable state, we're at the mercy of the people around us.

I did find that the psychedelic experience was unlike anything else, in my opinion. It was nothing like drinking alcohol. Since I hadn't tried anything else, I had no other basis for comparison. My experiences usually felt pretty brutal. The journeys were exhausting. Plus, part of the preparation for the ceremony was fasting which gave me a migraine nearly 100 percent of the time.

I remember a specific journey when my body tremored all day long. My legs shook as I walked to the bathroom, I was tossing and turning on my mat and I was covered in sweat. All I *saw* was darkness. This went on for nearly eight hours. About halfway through the journey it occurred to me these tremors were all the trauma leaving my body from the many beatings throughout my childhood and adolescence. The medicine was literally shaking the trauma from my body. I didn't have a migraine after that journey. There were some specific aches and pains that have never returned since that experience.

Ultimately, it was my lessons through plant medicines that helped me cure myself of migraines altogether. As with anything in life, there are pros and cons. Even through the physical misery of this process, I firmly believe this work saved my life.

So why would I put myself through this for several years? Well, it was because I actually was getting better. That said, I eventually left the group because I never felt safe with some of the people in the group. Not unsafe in terms of bodily safety, rather I felt emotionally unsafe. The experiences shared in this environment made me feel deeply vulnerable and comments others made when I was in that frame of mind were deeply painful and harmful.

For example, I was on the mat the day my mother passed away. In the evening I was exhausted and there were still several folks up and around. I found my phone so I could listen to music and drift off. As I powered up my phone, I knew this was a breach of the group's "container protocol." There was a standing rule that phones were prohibited from the time the ceremony opened to when it closed at the end of the weekend. Anyway, the landing screen was a text that my mother had passed that afternoon. I asked for a candle to light in honor of her passing.

Everyone present was aware of my non-relationship with my mother, so her death brought mixed reactions. Some said they hoped this would bring me some closure and eventually peace. Of course, I had to admit I had turned on my phone to find music only to see the text there. Most people didn't make much of my looking for music on my phone. But not everyone was kind, either. One person was quite angry that I had broken the rules and made it known to the group. It didn't matter what the news was. What mattered was that I broke the rules.

In hindsight, it's hilarious that a woman was badgering me for breaking the rules when the woman who had given birth to me and tortured me for 16 years had just died. One more swipe from the other side.

I'm not in contact with any of the group's members anymore. I've gone my own way, wished them the best, and moved on. In a way, that group was like a bubble containing a personal journey. Everyone was participating in that container's level of safety. It seemed like there were clear enough borders or boundaries for me. In the context of the larger experience of sharing, then spending the rest of the time with myself—my experiences and thoughts—it felt like it was worth the risk at the time. Along the way, I also was negotiating my own sense of hypocrisy and belief systems about the use of medicines. I was challenging the notion that these substances could be beneficial, healing, nurturing, and comforting.

To be clear, what I mean by *container* is the set of agreements holding the space together. Everyone agrees on which types of behaviors are acceptable and which ones are not. There's also the element of confidentiality and kindness to one another. A good facilitator creates a solid container in which the participants feel safe and can focus on their own internal journeys. Each facilitator has a personal way to create a container. And I cannot stress enough how important the facilitator and the container are to the integrity of the experience.

Due to my own conflicts and the controversies associated with the use of substances, the group experiences were a struggle for me. However, I noticed enough change within myself that I thought continuing to participate was a good decision. I did realize that the overall energy of the group was challenging for me, as well.

I learned from them in terms of how to be kind and gentle with people because we don't know where they are in their lives. We have no idea what someone has experienced when we pass them on the street or say hello to them in the grocery store. It's impossible to know what that person's life is like beneath the surface. That's how listening to the shared experiences of group members helped me to some degree. Importantly, it opened my eyes to see that, while the abuse I endured was awful, it wasn't unique. Many people in the group had suffered some truly horrific treatment at the hands of others. I was even a bit squeamish when I heard their stories, but this new perspective did help me.

Nevertheless, I didn't feel like I belonged in that group and was operating outside of what "normal" people had experienced. I saw what I thought was normal from the outside, yet it could have been just as horrific as my home was on the inside while growing up. How was I to know? I certainly wasn't telling anyone what was happening inside my home. I learned to avoid that at a young age. Why would anyone else be talking about such things?

The impact of this sharing changed what my sense of what normalcy was. I could say to myself that those experiences were not uncommon. I realized that I wasn't a pariah because of all the crazy stuff that happened to me. Yes, I've had some truly awful experiences, but so have a lot of other people. Oddly, there was freedom in realizing that—freedom in hearing other people's harrowing experiences. This didn't make my experiences less traumatic, but it made me feel less different. Sharing my experiences and theirs helped me feel whole.

I will say that the person I was when I entered that community was very different from the one who left years later. Prior to joining the group, I had no real self-respect or dignity. I didn't feel like I belonged anywhere or that I was a useful participant in society. I constantly wondered why I'd even been born or why I endured being here. It didn't make sense to me when I asked why I was here. I felt like I was bobbing away alone in the middle of the ocean.

The collective experience in that group helped me come ashore, in a sense. I could open my heart to others and share space with people in a non-combative, more peaceful way. That allowed me to have a much different connection to society as a whole. You know, that sense of collective experience that we're having all of the time where we live. I felt much more a part of that after my relationship with this particular group.

Next, I began working with a different facilitator, who I had met through a member of the group. This was a trained psychologist and plant medicine facilitator and most of our work together was one-on-one. This allowed us to work independently and address whatever was coming up for me at that time.

My relationship with this facilitator was magical. There was deep trust. I felt very safe with this person although a very different approach was used than the lie-on-the-mat medicine journey. It wasn't all hands-off, though. There were guided meditations, yoga movements, and other activities. There was actual work I could do during my journey to help heal my trauma. This involved re-experiencing some deeply traumatic moments in my life and being able to recontextualize them.

It was with this facilitator that I had a defining moment that forever changed me. In this transformational experience with my facilitator, I had my first and only influential visual psychedelic experience. It absolutely changed my life.

There I was, lying with my head on a pillow listening to music. My eyes were closed, with eyeshades on. I started seeing various shapes and forms begin to materialize, fall away, materialize, and fall away. They also were all different colors and sizes. There was no beginning and no end to what I saw. And the colors were bright and beautiful, something like fireworks. Interestingly, most of the shapes were geometric. I actually opened my eyes and made a joke asking, "So, this is what you guys mean by psychedelic?" We both laughed and I explained a little bit about what I was seeing.

I went back into my experience, seeing the shapes and colors again. But then there was nothing. Yet, it wasn't that nothing was there. I can only describe it as everything being there and nothing being there at the same time. It was a sort of an inside out feeling of knowing that I was part of the universe and the universe was part of me. I remember my head moving around on the pillow to see if I could find the end of it. But there was no end. It was everywhere. So, this was a truly profound experience.

That experience still makes me speechless because it was life changing. I could see with clarity that I had a place in the universe. I was part of something outside myself and I knew even in that state and in that moment that I'd never be the same again.

The reason why I recount this experience for you is because it was part of my journey and I want to tell my whole story. My goal is to help you understand that the depth of my suffering is what ultimately led me in this direction with the use of plant medicines.

I believe I was fortunate to be involved with people of integrity with regard to the medicines. It's important to remember if you're going to use such substances, you must have the ceremony, the ritual, and the container. It's essential to work with someone for whom you have deep respect and trust. This choice is not to be trivialized or be trifled with. It's a remarkably transformative process that should only be entered into with deep respect and reverence for it, the medicine, and yourself. I sensed that level of respect, so the experience was life changing. I even felt gratitude for the experience as well as the knowledge it gave me. It made me finally feel a sense of peace.

I couldn't have had that experience alone in a vacuum. It took all of the work that preceded it to be manifested. And I do mean all of the work, including the books, seminars, coaches, people I'd met, therapists, counselors, friends, and colleagues. It required the entire body of my work to reach that point, to have that moment, to have that experience, and to allow myself to be changed by it.

It would be easy for me to speculate about which other methodologies or tools I could've used to take me the same distance over the same period of time. But I don't know the answer to that. Actually, I don't believe it's worth speculating about. I made a big decision. I'm grateful for it and for all the ways it has changed my life.

These are changes that I firmly believe saved my life. They've allowed me the space to do the work on my physical and mental well-being to prevent me from having a stroke or heart attack. I have the space to use acupuncture to aid my internal systems, I can regulate my cortisol levels and therefore normalize my sleep-wake cycle so I can have healthy circadian rhythms. Basically, these tools were effective in helping my healing take place.

Over about a five-year period, none of my other medicine journeys were psychedelic in nature. I often didn't have any memories of them. I had glimpses, feelings, intuitions, or a sense that something in me had changed. I recognized that an automatic behavior had changed.

I liken this to going outside and taking the same path every day. The shrubbery on the path is all worn down where you take your steps and it's high on the sides. You always can see the path. That's the pattern or habit, as you don't even think about following the path. But one time, that path is gone. All of the sudden, you now stand at a decision point because that well-worn path is gone. You have the freedom to choose a different direction because the pattern is no longer there.

That's what I noticed through the medicine journeys more than anything else. My automatic behaviors changed. The paths were no longer there. I spent more of my time choosing how I wanted to respond to given situations. This included how I wanted to show up for work, for my friends, and for a romantic partner. I was finally making choices. And it was tremendously liberating to feel a sense of control to decide for myself based on my own wants, needs, and desires.

I now felt at peace making decisions about things that could be explored and experienced as if for the first time. This was possible because the automatic behavioral patterns were gone. It's a beautiful thing to be able to make choices.

I suppose that a big takeaway for me is that I feel incredibly lucky to have had these opportunities brought to my attention and made available to me. And I'm grateful to all the people I met along the way. I learned something from every one of them, either through shared experiences or their narrative about their own lives.

Chapter 12
My Coaching Experience –
Sticks and Stones

Just so you know, I use the term "Sticks and Stones" in this chapter's title in a tongue and cheek kind of way. The saying, "Sticks and stones may break my bones, but words will never harm me" is so inaccurate. Let me explain.

Approximately two years after my first problematic engagement with a life coach, I was introduced to a woman whose spell I fell under immediately. I attended a medicine ceremony at her temple. The way she worked with people there and her energy was amazing. There was an energy and level of interaction I wanted to model. At the time I was pursuing my coaching certificate, so it also was relevant to my studies.

During the ceremony this coach talked a lot about personal sovereignty and not giving your power away to others. These were topics that were deeply important to me. As an abused child, I was taught to give my power away to anyone I felt was "better than I was." Years of behavior patternmaking made me believe that everyone was better than I was. I was accustomed to being subservient to anyone in my orbit whom I perceived as being in a position of power.

Because this coach's approach resonated with me, I ended up spending quite a bit of money for those services. I admit that I put this coach on a pedestal. I thought part of being coached was to learn this professional's ways and be more like that person. Looking back, this ended up being another case of my external focus of wanting to fit in and appearing like those around me so it was easier to belong.

Clearly, I went into the coaching engagement for all the wrong reasons. It began because I was referred to this coach, which was fine. However, my fascination with this individual set the tone for what was to be an unhealthy relationship.

I now know that a coaching relationship should never feel like one person is superior or inferior to the other. The coach should be providing tools and techniques and helping to identify the aspects that resonate with and are sustainable for the client. After all, different tools and techniques resonate in different ways with different people. There isn't a one-size-fits-all approach in the coaching world. It's just not possible.

I didn't begin our coaching engagement with a clear understanding about the tools or methodology to be employed—or even how this relationship was going to help me. I didn't take the time to research this coach. That would include analyzing the coaches website content and body work. I didn't even determine if this coach's specialty was related to what I was trying to work on. I was somewhat bowled over by our first meeting and went headlong into the coaching engagement.

As it turned out, this coach was incredibly unprofessional and I didn't benefit from the relationship. That was jarring to me, especially the way the connection ended. I actually felt beat up a few times after sessions. Sadly, during the coaching engagement I never spoke up for myself to say, "Hey, I don't really appreciate the way you're talking to me. I don't appreciate the way you're phrasing that. You're hurting my feelings by the way you're talking to me. What you're saying isn't resonating with me. What we're doing just isn't working."

I felt terribly trapped during the entire engagement partly because I'd paid a lot of money for it. I was obviously invested on a financial level, but also on a personal, emotional level. Nevertheless, I wasn't getting any benefit from this engagement because I wasn't learning how to use tools and techniques to move forward in a healthy way.

A case in point during a particular session this coach seemed very frustrated with me, looked me straight in the eye and said, "You just need to lighten the fuck up."

That remark felt like getting punched in the face—and I know the feeling of having been punched in the face by my mother. I thought, "Wow! This person who's supposed to be providing a safe space for me, making me feel empowered, and caring for me just told me to lighten the fuck up." I'm not sure what sort of therapeutic relationship would make it appropriate for a statement like that to be acceptable. I certainly didn't find it acceptable. Yet I froze because I didn't feel like I could say anything. I was traumatized by that attack. Admittedly, I held on to quite a bit of resentment about how I was treated and the way that I wasn't coached.

Several months later she reached out to me to ask if I had been negatively impacted by one of her partners or other healers in her network. Apparently one of her colleagues had offended a number of her clients and she was trying to make amends. I was quite proud of myself, I explained it was she who had injured me by the way she had treated me. Yes, I had finally found my voice in the moment when it mattered. I was shaking from head to toe, but I stood my ground and expressed my disappointment with her behavior toward me. This was a personal victory for me.

I share this experience mostly as what not to do if you're in an engagement with a professional, especially if that person does something you find offensive or hurtful. You must find a way to communicate your reaction to what's going on, whether you email it, text it, or if you feel safe enough to talk about it. Your response needs to come out so you can continue to benefit from that engagement or determine that you should end it. Either way, embracing self-advocacy, standing up with your own power, and having your boundaries set helps to prevent a coach from violating those boundaries.

One other hard earned lesson, I was participating in a training session being delivered by a different coach than mentioned above. I was very surprised to learn about a particular approach this coach followed. I was told that when clients called, texted, or emailed messages, no response would occur for several hours or maybe even a day. This coach's rationale was that people needed to learn to become more independent and resourceful. As a client, I was absolutely appalled by this statement. The week before, I was one of those clients leaving a tearful message, asking to speak, and not getting a response for a couple of days. That was my coach telling me to "buck up" by not responding to me. And then to hear this coach tell the story to our class, the arrogance and lack of empathy was breathtaking.

It's fine if this is an agreed upon approach between you and your coach. However, it could be very problematic in an emergency when guidance is required immediately. The lesson here is that it's important for both parties to understand and agree on the approach and expectations before starting a relationship.

Consider this: Any time you're in a professional engagement, hold the person you're working with accountable when it comes to the framework upon which you've agreed to work together. This is your sacred journey. It's your story. It's your time. And you deserve to be treated with respect, dignity, and kindness. It must be a beneficial and sustainable relationship. You should never accept less.

Chapter 13
Finding Balance and Happiness

Our happiness is a balancing act. The reality is that nobody is happy or angry one hundred percent of the time. Our emotions pass through us like weather patterns. It's perfectly normal to want the "happy" state of mind more than less comfortable emotions. However, they're all passing states of being.

As a human being, you have control over your emotional state. If you're feeling down, you can cheer up by listening to your favorite song, going for a walk outside, taking three deep belly breaths, or drinking some water. Afterward, observe your state. It seems like your mood can magically change!

The lesson is that we don't need to become locked into any one state. Instead we just need to observe them as they move through us, much as we observe a rainstorm, a full moon, or a rainbow appear and fade away. What we want is equilibrium. Performing acts of self-kindness at a conscious level will give us more balance in our day-to-day life so we can respond to situations versus only reacting to them.

Chances are that you'll experience moments when you can say, "Wow, what that person said really triggered me and I can't figure out why." You acknowledge that moment for what it is rather than trying to come up with something you can say to hurt that person's feelings just because trigger words upset you. This less reactive type of response makes your relationships better and your nervous system more balanced. You feel better at the end of the day.

If you're more conscious of what's happening, you should have fewer impulses to beat yourself up over how you reacted to triggers. This allows you to put a pin in that experience and think about it later when you're taking some time to work out why that situation was so emotionally trying.

Remember that the important element in maintaining balance is how you experience what others say and what it touches in your unconscious that triggers you. That's it. Most likely those people have no idea what they're doing or saying. Even if they hurt you, there's a good chance it isn't on purpose. However, when people are suffering their automatic behavior can be to strike out at others to avoid the pain they're experiencing. Knowing this, you can respond differently because you have a different perspective. You can take what they say less personally when you interact with them. The moment can be less about you, which allows you to feel compassion for them knowing they may always be angry or unhappy.

Can you imagine being angry all the time? That can't be a good way to live. Just know that it's within those other people. You're not making them angry. It's their state of being, their inner turmoil. Since it's impossible to fully know someone else's experience and state of mind, it's best to offer compassion. You can't change what another person says or thinks. However, you can try to diffuse the situation by responding with compassion.

Let's face it, there are people who seem to always be angry, bitter, or very negative. We don't have to take what they say personally because that's how they always are. That's how they talk to everyone. It's a reflection of who they are on the inside, not whom they're talking to.

For example, my mother was constantly angry. Even when she was laughing, she was angry. As I look back, it's confusing why she always was in a fit of rage. Even when drunk, she was angry. It's inexplicable to me because she never worked. She had everything handed to her and her two eldest children loved and doted on her unconditionally.

No one ever told us about people like that when we were children or even older. We could've been taught to look at somebody else's behavior as an extension of his or her own experience, rather than as a reflection of whom they believe we were at that moment. Understanding that we're all reacting from our own set of experiences and responding based on those is a tremendously liberating thing.

This is acknowledging the fact that none of us can know what's happening inside others' minds or what their set of life experiences have been. Based on that awareness, we're able to establish a perspective that comes from our self-kindness, consciousness, and compassion for others. That's so we don't operate from a place where everything is our fault or due to our flaws. Sounds easy, right?

I still struggle with this idea of not taking cruel words personally. My entire childhood was riddled with everything that was wrong, bad, and disappointing about me. Now in my adulthood, how in the world am I magically not supposed to take things personally? We're even more vulnerable to cruelty, particularly these days with the anonymity of the internet. Wow, people can be vicious when they're alone behind their keyboards. Someone with wounded self-esteem might have zero experience dealing with people projecting their anger toward others. Vulnerable recipients of anger-riddled messages, posts, and such communications are conditioned to believe it must be them at fault.

All I can say is to expect coping with attacks of this nature to be a work in progress. As an empath I can feel the emotions of others. After much training and observation of my own emotions, I'm now mostly able to tell when disturbing emotions belong to someone else. So, I'm not surprised if someone becomes abusive or belligerent, nor do I take it personally. That's to say, my feelings might briefly get bruised, but I'm able to put the situation in context and allow the hurt feelings to move on.

I suggest that you come up with a coping mechanism for yourself, particularly if you have a sensitive nature. Devise a method to use in the moment to get yourself centered. The most important piece is not to engage with those coming from negative places. Allow the "storm" to pass so you can determine what, if anything, needs to be done for resolution.

It's deeply empowering when you can stand firm in a tense situation, remain calm and centered, and then respond with grace. This also can have a domino effect internally and externally because changes to related behavior patterns may be set in motion. That is, once this becomes your new pattern you are operating from a place of balance and inner peace which positively affects you and will also affect those around you.

Chapter 14
Laundry Chute

Here's one of the most profound things I've come to understand through my self-discovery and healing journey. It's this: At a certain point in our life it would have served us well if someone had pulled us aside and told us it's critical that we allow ourselves to forget nearly everything we'd ever been told and believed about ourselves, society, and the world. In other words, throw all of your old beliefs down the laundry chute to be refreshed.

This new intelligent innocence would begin the next chapter of our life, whether it be after graduating high school or college or just heading off to "real life." At this inflection point, we might have come to better understand who we were and what we wanted, needed, enjoyed, didn't like, and what we wanted or didn't want out of life.

Through our infancy and youth, we're indoctrinated by the culture of our immediate family: what they believed, how they felt, who they liked, what they ate, what they celebrated, and what they approved of. All their behavior patterns and the way they interacted with one another, as well as their situations in life, rubbed off on us. We had no alternative story to the one that we grew up in and experienced. I don't say this is a negative thing, it's just a fact that we grow up around a group of people, immediate family or otherwise, and we are constantly exposed to their belief systems.

It isn't until we're teenagers when we typically begin to see the world from a different perspective. Often this is when we start thinking about how we want our world to look as we grow older. We begin to add different facets to our lives based on what we already experienced and have come to believe.

We may have been told what we should want in terms of our family culture. In some cultures, arranged marriages are expected. You're simply told whom to marry. To stay in your culture and in your family, you follow that tradition. There are many cultures around the world in which certain expectations like this are required to stay within the family construct. Whether or not that resonates with you is immaterial. It's just expected and that's how life goes.

Those are the lenses through which we see life present itself related to our family home and our world. They're projected on everything around us and guide our behaviors and our beliefs. They direct our actions, interactions, relationships, and even how we operate at our jobs.

There are societal expectations, as well. We go to school. We graduate. We get a job. In some cultures, there is a certain type of job we're expected to seek. We get married and we have kids. We play our role in this story. But too often, we don't ask if we want to get married, want to have children, or question the professional path we want to follow.

Expectations are heaped on us. And that's not necessarily just by family because we're now swept up in the avalanche of social media. The expectations are tenfold due to this constant and often conflicting messaging. Admittedly, it's quite different now from when I was a child, as we didn't have social media—not even smartphones and computers to connect us with others 24/7/365. That's the added dimension young people must sort through these days.

In my life I didn't agree with, believe in, or want to emulate anything that my family of origin stood for. They were incredibly abusive to everyone. They weren't contributing members of society. They were prejudiced and racist. They led with hatred, animosity, and entitlement. Consequently, my entire childhood was framed by this abrasive edge. All I wanted to do was love everybody and all my family wanted to do was destroy everything.

The result when I was out in the world was that I knew everything I'd been taught was wrong. But I had nothing to fill that empty space. Therefore, over the years I just started scraping together different ways of being and living. Until my red light moment, my life still embodied the projections, behavior patterns, and things that had been foisted upon me as a child.

What I'm trying to say is it would behoove us to know that unless we've already spent a tremendous amount of time unwinding ourselves from our family systems it's hard to come to terms with who we are at a fundamental, foundational level. I mean that in a broad sense. In other words, what do we really believe?

Try stepping back and examining the belief systems that brought you to this point. Whether it's an issue, circumstance, event, or experience, look at it from your own perspective and figure out how you really feel about it. Don't just assess your ingrained or immediate reactions. Look at two or three reactions after that. What do you see if you continue to ask yourself, "How do I feel about this on multiple levels?"

This is when you start peeling back the layers of everyone else's belief systems and behavior patterns so you can get down to the layer of your original or core self. It's how you acknowledge your true nature. This is where your innermost self resides to authentically deal with how you feel about something or how you react to any given situation.

Over the years, I've even told my clients that they would benefit from gathering up all those beliefs that were gifted to them by other people and throw them down the laundry chute. That's how they could start over on their own terms. This way, they could begin to know themselves and begin to understand themselves at a deeper level.

Do you think you could begin to understand what's beneath your thoughts and reactions? Would you even agree with what you find there? Would you believe in that? Would it be true to you? Would it be your true nature, structure, or outcome of the belief systems and patterns you were raised with?

Importantly, I don't suggest that we throw all our structures and beliefs in the garbage. That's why I chose the metaphor of a laundry chute. It's because within the belief systems and behavior patterns imposed upon us, as well as within our own belief systems, is true wisdom… your true wisdom. Think of this as unhooking the emotional reactionary attachment part of it. What you hold onto is the wisdom, understanding, and knowing parts. So, it's like the laundry chute leads to washing away all the stains and muck of the attachments, leaving the "clean laundry" to wear.

As an example, my mother walked physically and mentally with defiance. It was as if she dared anyone to get in her way, say something she didn't like, or commit some other offense she interpreted as a slight. In contrast, I seek out eye contact with people so I can smile at them. I tend to compliment random strangers because they have cute hair or are wearing a fun piece of clothing. If they seem emotionally down, I want to show them some kindness. I do exactly the opposite of what was modeled for me by my mother. I use my inner knowing that people want to be treated with respect. In other words, I've cleaned up the behavior of my mother by choosing to extend kindness.

Another way of looking at this shedding of the unhealthful attachments is to consider the noise—internal and external—that stands in the way of being able to get in touch with yourself and your own wisdom. This means both organic wisdom and learned wisdom accumulated throughout your lifetime. Without those attachments, you can be much more grounded and far truer to yourself as you react and behave in life.

Your experiences become better, lighter, more engaging, and more joyful because you're operating from a place of true strength. You're experiencing life from a place of your deepest, truest self. From that place you can uncover your peace and your bliss. You can find your own navigation and recognize your own internal awareness of your own voice. Furthermore, you can unveil your own ability to direct your life, to keep experiencing that sense of your true nature, of joy, bliss, and peace.

As you do this, you show those around you that organic joy from being yourself. You'll notice that your enjoyment is quite contagious as it reinforces those feelings around you. Moreover, this way of relating to yourself becomes the voice of your own best friend, your own mentor, the person—your true self—that you want to check in with before making decisions. It gives you the strength to have a power that comes from within. It doesn't require the acceptance of others. You don't need someone else to tell you this or that is the right thing to do or what you should do. It's because now that you're in touch with your true nature, you can direct yourself as that confidant, best friend, and deep knowing voice that guides you in the right direction.

Living aligned with your true nature, the people in your life become a joy to you. They become a wonder with whom to share that sort of organic true nature. That's because they're very likely moving in the same direction as well. In life, like attracts like. As you change dimensionally, change your frequency, and change your inner persona, the people in your life morph and change respectively. Again, like attracts like and frequencies attract frequencies.

Now as you move through these frequencies, you'll begin to move and circle in on the community of people operating at that same frequency. That will create harmony. This continues to be enhanced once you have a sense of self and of self-direction. The curiosity never ends. The thirst is never quenched. There'll always be a desire to do more, learn more, and understand more. And it's no longer a job or work or a healing journey at that point. It's actually just a constant source of self-discovery. And that's a pretty amazing place to be.

Chapter 15
Sammy

I recently encountered a force of nature: Grief. I felt grief that was more powerful than all the trauma I'd experienced combined in terms of the emotional impact. I thought I'd experienced grief before, but what I believe I experienced was more a feeling of loss.

My initial brush with grief was the passing of one of my favorite people in the whole world, my cousin Louie. He lived with my family for a short time. Years ago, I remember thinking that what I was feeling about his loss was grief. At his funeral, I said there was a brighter star in the sky now that he was gone. This was because he was the only member of my near or extended family whom I really loved. He had a heart of gold and was the kindest, gentlest, most wonderful person. He was taken far too young.

Since then, more family members have passed. My mother, my sister, and tragically my young nephew. In those cases, I did mourn the loss but it was different. I'd lived with them, had shared in their suffering, and had been at the mercy of my mother's suffering too many times to count.

There also was a part of me that was actually relieved that they were no longer suffering. Every day they were here on Earth, they suffered deeply. I viewed their deaths almost as a humane outcome. It's like when someone is terminally ill and all they're experiencing is pain management. You desperately want that person to no longer endure that suffering. So, in large part, that's how I felt when my immediate family members passed. Admittedly in some cases, I felt slightly jealous that their suffering was over and mine wasn't.

With those deaths, I believed I had experienced grief. That was until more recently one of my dogs, Sam, died. Or as I liked to call him, Sammy the Bammy. My husband and I adopted Sam from a family that was about to have a child and couldn't take care of him. He was a sweet little dog, part Corgi. When Sam was excited, he would spin around in circles. When he barked, all four feet would come off the ground—it was so adorable. His whole body would bounce when he'd go to the door to greet my husband. Sam was a wonderful, good natured little dog who brought us a lot of joy.

When we adopted Sam, Charlie had been with us for a couple of years. I was used to a dog like Charlie who kept to himself, liked to play fetch, and was playful but wasn't necessarily a cuddler. He wasn't much of a lap dog. Sam on the other hand was a huge cuddler. I remember the first night he stayed with us when his previous owners brought him to our house. That evening, he came running down the stairs, sped across the living room floor, and jumped onto my lap. It was adorable how he put his paws on my shoulders. Sam had this big smile on his face, it was like he was thanking me for giving him a home.

I quickly learned that Sam would be a real people lover. He loved to cuddle and curl up on or near me. If I sat cross-legged on the ground, he'd curl up in my legs. If I sat on the couch, he'd rest his head on my knee with one of his legs across my leg. He'd just hang out this way and sleep with me.

We had Sam in our lives for five years. About a year and a half into him living with us, he had a seizure. He didn't lose consciousness during the episode. My husband and I were with him at the time. We didn't think he was physically harmed, but we consulted a vet anyway. One of the things the vet recommended was to change the flea and tick medication we used because there was a small risk of seizures. After that, Sam never had another major seizure again, only a few minor episodes when he zoned out for a few seconds and didn't seem to know what was going on.

During his regular exam, the vet checked Sam's teeth and found that many of them were smaller than they should've been. They were wearing down and he was having some issues with his gums. The vet recommended pulling the teeth because they weren't his chewing teeth. The removal of those teeth wouldn't interfere with his ability to eat but that would stop the deterioration of his gums. We also found out that Sam had gone blind.

We didn't want Sam to be in pain, so we scheduled the surgery. He went through his pre-op appointments and was given a green light for the procedure. Sam came through the surgery fine. After he arrived home, he was still dizzy and not his normal self due to the medication. About a week later, the day after my birthday, Sam and Charlie were sleeping in beds on our bedroom floor. I heard Sam shuffling around so I checked on him, especially in case he needed to go outside. He seemed quite confused, scared, and could only turn in circles. Yet, nothing else was visibly wrong with him, such as experiencing spasms. So, I sat with him and he folded his body into my lap. I just let him sleep there where he could feel safe and content.

This situation continued the next day. We had to carry him outside. He was quiet and lethargic as well. He just wasn't himself. We figured that he likely had a seizure during his sleep.

As it turned out, we had to make the decision to let Sam go. My husband found a way to have the procedure performed at our house. This way, we didn't have to be in a sterile room to say goodbye to our dear family member. The night before, we all slept on the couch together so Sam would know he was loved and that we were right there. I remember waking up in the middle of the night just to just look at him. He had rolled over and put his head on my husband's shoulder. It was so beautiful to see that. I remember just sitting and watching him sleep. Somewhere inside of me, I was starting to understand that Sam was going to be taken away. I just wanted to look at him and touch him as much as I could.

That morning, we cooked him his favorite breakfast. Later, the professional came to handle Sam's procedure and was fantastic, clearly understanding the depth of people's sadness as they said goodbye to a family member like this. We went through the procedure and did everything that we needed to do. That was, we held Sam, told him how much we loved him, and how we were grateful for the five years he was with us. We told him that he would always be part of our family. When he was gone, I pulled him onto my lap. I just wanted to hold him and to touch him.

I was in such unbearable pain. But I understood that doing this for Sam was the right, unselfish, and humane thing to do because he was suffering. He wasn't able to do normal activities and had lost his vision. In my heart, we knew that wasn't an acceptable quality of life for him.

What I'd come to understand over the next few days was that grief is a force of nature that splits you open and tears you apart. I'd never felt such a force, such deep pain in my body. I knew from all the work I'd been doing on myself over the past several years that I needed to allow myself to experience this pain and to extend some compassion to myself.

Several people encouraged me to hurry up and adopt another dog to fill the hole that Sam left. But I couldn't. First of all, nothing could ever fill the hole that Sam had just left. I felt that it would be deeply disrespectful to his memory to just try to insert another dog in his place. I wanted to respect and honor this little creature, this little being who had enriched and changed my life.

You see, Sam had been abused. We could tell when he first came to us, how he would cower when we had things in our hands. This was utterly heartbreaking. Sam was only about 16 pounds and had tiny legs. He wasn't built to be able to defend himself. It was so awful to think that somebody could hurt this wonderful little being.

I quickly realized that Sam and I bonded because we both had been abused. As a result, you sometimes forget that you exist because you've been discarded, rejected, and abandoned so often. There are times when you need someone to remind you that you're real. I could feel that need in Sam in the same way I began to understand that need in myself. He and I really resonated on that level.

In the days following his death, it was as if a bomb had gone off inside me. I knew I'd never be the same. I was understanding the fragility of life on a different level. That was interesting for someone like me who had swung back and forth between not wanting to be alive anymore and then finding purpose in life. I believe the experience of losing Sam both crushed and opened my heart. Yet, there was a beauty in that experience because it connected me with a place in my heart I'd never been in touch with before. It definitely changed the way I see the connectedness of people and animals… and everything.

I offer this experience as another type of transformational moment you can arrive at when there is an immediate requirement for change. It doesn't necessarily take a traumatic childhood, bad relationship, or an abusive situation to spark deep grief. It can be due to the loss of something or someone. It can be initiated by something you don't even understand. But you definitely know the depth of your feelings when that close relationship is no longer there.

Joni Mitchell sings the lyrics, "You don't know what you've got 'til it's gone," It's true because even though we may deeply love and honor people or beings while they're alive, we may discover there are additional depths to our love. This can present itself in ways we weren't aware of before. It can give us the capacity to recognize those greater depths of love are deeply rooted in our relationships.

If you experience a devastating loss in your life, you may find yourself at a crossroads. It's where all of a sudden you need to make some big decisions about who you are, what you want, and what comes next. All the same rules apply no matter what experience brings you to this crossroad. My point is that you need to get in touch with your internal counselor to figure out what's best for you at that point. What do you need? What will it take for you to go where you want to be next? What direction do you need to go to find your joy and peace?

I guess the best way I can describe this process is to just let it unfold. For me with regard to Sam, the first few days were incredibly intense. The evening we let him go when I was feeding Charlie, it was just heartbreaking to see Sam's bowl empty. Even the word heartbreaking doesn't seem to be a strong enough word for the pain I felt.

Nevertheless, I just allowed the process to unfold in whatever ways it was going to. Some days were relatively normal. But other days I broke down crying multiple times. I sat and stared at pictures of Sam and held his blanket.

I still have his blanket in my office where I can see it every day, as well as one of his favorite toys on my nightstand with his collar around it. His memory and presence are alive in me all the time. I think that's the case because I allowed myself to experience the pain of his loss. I didn't try to bypass it, replace him, or attempt other avoidance techniques. I believe this is because I deeply loved him and wanted to respect his passing.

It's for these reasons I think it's important to allow our natural processes to unfold. There's a fine line here, though. If the process results in neuroses or debilitating grief, you could become deeply depressed or possibly worse. So, there's a balance in not trying to bypass the situation and not overindulging in it either. I don't see overindulging as a choice necessarily. I do see it as getting deeply caught up in grief and unable to pull out of it. At that point, it's best to seek professional help so that depression doesn't turn into something worse.

In my experience with very deep grief, I found it to be similar to many of the traumatic experiences I'd had as a child, collectively. Obviously, this other type of grief wasn't the result of the horrendous, violent, abusive types of traumas. However, the force of that pain and loss in grief was every bit as palpable and strong as the force of the pain, anger, and rage due to all the beatings and terrible things that were said and done to me.

However, you don't necessarily need to be triggered by a terrible childhood to have your world rocked to the point where it changes you as a person. There's more than one way to arrive at this place of profound grief. It's that point where you suddenly need to focus inward. It's when you start healing yourself, as well as your wounds, behavior patterns, and belief systems so you can reach a more peaceful, hopeful, joyful place in your life.

I don't want to give the impression that to experience this level of trauma, you need to have been abused. You can have one situation occur that results in an equal amount of trauma for you. That doesn't diminish what may have happened to someone else in any way. And it's important that we understand on a very deep level that others' experiences are personal and their reactions to those experiences are their own. They're based on a constellation of things happening inside them in their unique environments. As someone on the outside, you can never fully understand what another person has experienced or is going through, just as they can never totally understand your personal history.

You need to offer yourself some gentleness when applying your definition of what your trauma means to you. That is, not allowing someone on the outside to explain the meaning of your trauma to you. They can't tell you how big or little it is, nor what you should or shouldn't do about it.

This is what I mean by the rules regarding coping with deep grief and trauma. These rules apply at all your crossroads. Come back to yourself, back to your internal counselor and find out what you need at that point. What's that very first thing you need? That first step can help you start moving, because only you can answer the question about what you need. No one else is ever going to be able to give you the answer to that question. It takes time and patience. But there comes a point when you'll connect with your inner counselor, sense of intuition, and sense of knowing.

This is where you feel one hundred percent aligned with yourself, with respect to where you're going and what you're doing. It's knowing that you're taking steps to get there. This sounds so simple. Yet, I understand how this process can take a lot of time. One step can feel like you're pushing water uphill with a fork. It's two steps forward, a few steps back. Trust that there's always a first step forward, a next step, and another one after that. Honestly, that's all you can ever do at any given time. Just take the next step.

I suppose the step taking metaphor fits me because I'm an avid walker. And it's quite appropriate with regard to coping with my loss of Sam. Invariably I run into many dogs when I'm out walking. I always catch my breath when I see dogs that look like Sam. My tummy gets a little tight, but I always ask their owners if I can say hello. If I'm allowed, I stoop down to pet and talk with them. Sometimes their faces and ears remind me of Sam. He had the most amazing ears. They would stand straight up when he was paying attention or excited about something. We called them his little satellite dishes. Sometimes I mention that to the owners and usually get a good chuckle.

We have a hand-painted portrait of Sam hanging in our kitchen. It was given to us as a gift from my sister-in-law. I say hello to him every morning. Sam remains very close to my heart. I still feel the grief from losing Sam but it has changed and likely will keep changing as the years go by. I think that's true about any profound grief we experience. I urge you to come to understand the grief that affects you so you too can make peace with it.

Chapter 16
Your Place of Peace

I love the beach. I've always loved the beach. One of my earliest memories is standing on the porch of a house looking out over the water off the southern Texas coast. Even at that early age, I appreciated the enormity of the water and its power. Something really resonated with me about such a vast expanse of water and the fact that I couldn't see the end of it. It made me feel like there was something bigger going on than what I could see. I believe that was my first experience of peace.

Being near the ocean calms the seemingly endless whirlwind of what goes on in my head and all around me. For this reason, the beach remains a very powerful place for me to clear my mind and just... be.

Having a place of peace like that is a key to maintaining any kind of hope so you're then able to overcome situations. This state of mind involves being able to see situations from a perspective that allows you some space to see around it, over it, or through it, depending on how you contextualize the situations for yourself. I encourage you not to become overwhelmed with your thoughts, feelings, or life either. Find someplace or something that allows you to pull yourself out of those chaotic places in your head.

One thing I've said throughout my coaching career and even in my business management work. It's that if you're angry, you're not thinking rationally. You've got to help yourself move past the anger before making matters worse, both internally and externally. One trick is to create a list of actions you can take to make yourself feel better from the perspective of a more peaceful state. Of course, those actions might change depending on which emotion you're experiencing. If you feel angry, you may have one set of actions that help. But if you're sad, it may be a completely different set of actions that will help you.

It's important to have an array of strategies that work for you for different types of situations. For example, I can't go to a beach every time I want to so I use music as a tool to shift my state. If I'm frustrated, I march into my living room, turn on YouTube, and play the song from the singer Pink titled "Perfect" (the explicit version). I blast that song through the whole house. And by the time it's over, I might be crying but I'm calm. I'm able to look at the situation more openly and rationally because my perspective comes from compassion and with all the judgment removed.

Maybe you're angry, depressed, crying, or raging. It's an extremely uncomfortable place. And you know that no one is coming to rescue you from those feelings or that experience. This isn't about external circumstances, rather what's going on inside your body. You may feel overwhelmed about one thing, an accumulation of various types of things, or everything. It could be about work, friendships, something at home, or several things combined.

However, it also could be a situation within yourself in which you're battling yourself over something you want to do, have, or become. Whatever it is, it's causing you to experience a great deal of internal resistance. You may struggle to see that anything is progressing or being resolved. That can pull you into what I call *the spiral*. Your thoughts and emotions become a hamster wheel because they continually reinforce and multiply the same unproductive thoughts. This is when we tend to say, "I can't. I can't do it. I'm not worthy. I should just give up."

Just fill in what your inner critic or hamster wheel makes you think. What messages start coming through to you when that spiral begins? Do you feel yourself moving away from the moment you're experiencing and becoming consumed by all of the self-doubt, negativity, and recrimination? I describe this reaction as pulling out the sledgehammer and beating yourself to death. It's all too common. Please set down the sledgehammer. Nothing good will come from it.

So, what can you do in those moments when that sense of being overwhelmed sets in? Maybe you can't venture off to a place that's peaceful or rejuvenating for you, such as the beach, mountains, or park. In that case, you'll need to find other strategies to get yourself back to equilibrium, a state of rational thinking and clarity. This would be a state of mind in which you re-establish the ability to make good decisions and see situations from different perspectives.

When I'm upset, I might go for a walk, turn on music, or do some breathing exercises. There have been times when I'd drop to the floor and do 10 pushups. I might avoid that one if I'm around other people, as it could result in quite the unusual conversations afterward. The key is to break my pattern of thinking.

As I've said many times, no one is coming to rescue you or teach you how to be happy. It's simply not happening. This situation requires you to take the time to get to know yourself and to work through your issues and patterns. That's so you can reach a state of peace, happiness, and that sense of being you. I don't want to call this feeling "whole" necessarily, because that's not really what I'm talking about here. A state of wholeness implies that everything you want has come together or you crossed the finish line. I'm referring to reaching a healthy, happy operating state so you can move forward and effectively overcome life's challenges.

Basically what I'm saying is that I encourage you to just take one step in a new direction and then another step and then another to find your place of peace. Eventually you'll find the next action or resource that helps you and on to the next step. You never need to look back. Just keep moving forward, despite what life throws at you.

Chapter 17
The Gift of Awareness –
Making the Unconscious Conscious

Spiritual leader and author Eckhart Tolle often talks about the power of being in the present moment, as this is our only opportunity to truly change our behavior or habits. We cannot change a conversation that happened yesterday, and tomorrow isn't here to provide us with the gift of hindsight. Therefore, we're back to the present moment.

From the perspective of the present moment, have you ever considered how many activities in your life are managed by an unconscious pattern? Often, people say they don't want to know what's going on behind the scenes in their minds because they assume it's all negative. Think about it though, we all have good and bad habits so there must be good and healthy patterns present as well.

For a moment, consider how many completely unconscious actions each day make your life easier. Perhaps you set up the coffee pot the night before so it's ready to go first thing in the morning. Maybe you pre-pack your lunch. You unconsciously perform these tasks because you're aware enough of your tendencies to know you prefer to move more slowly in the morning without too many tasks. Taking a different perspective, these actions also could be viewed as acts of self-kindness—forms of self-care. You might frame such tasks by saying that you have your coffee ready, so you don't have to worry about it. You have your lunch ready, so that's not a bother in the morning. All that's taken care of because you've addressed it the night before. Taking these tasks off your mind before bed contributes to a more restful night's sleep.

That said, you don't perform these tasks unconsciously because you're a deficient person in any way. This is more about you taking care of yourself and understanding the way you behave. You learn to take actions that support yourself based on the way you behave. Obviously, these are good patterns and not self-destructive ones. What matters is how you explain these little things to yourself and how you make them conscious acts.

We also have the responsibility to ourselves to toss the habits and patterns that aren't serving us well. We should replace them with supportive habits and patterns. That's a big part of living consciously and intentionally.

So, don't be afraid to make the unconscious conscious. There are gems and marvelous things about you that are unconscious. Perhaps you thank someone without even having to think about the right social cue in the moment. Maybe when you hear someone sneeze you automatically say, "Bless you" or

"Gesundheit." Neither of these habits can be construed as negative.

So, it's not just all your bad habits and all the terrible things that happen to you that are rooted in your unconscious. They're present but maintaining a balance with what is conscious and not is critical. If you're not in balance with what lies in your unconscious, you run the risk of being triggered and possibly over-reacting to events. Then the unhealthful self-shaming and guilt process begins.

Please remember that we are at our most powerful when we are in the present moment, acknowledging what's going on in a conscious way.

Chapter 18
Random Acts of Self-Kindness That You Never Knew You Were Doing

It's Friday and you've had a challenging week at work or home. Perhaps you have a habit of taking a bath with some bubbles or bath salts in the evening. You pour a glass of wine, play your favorite music, or even sprinkle some flower petals in the water.

This is an example of performing a random act of kindness for yourself. Just because such acts might be less than fully intentional, don't stop doing them. Rather, make them conscious, intentional acts.

How can you do this? As you run your bath, put in the oils or salts, select your music, light some candles, and get your beverage of choice, intentionally understand that you're preparing a special environment for yourself. You're creating a place of softness, beauty, and kindness for yourself. The intention is to have a warm bath to help your body relax. The oils provide fragrance, moisturizers soothe your skin, and the music calms your mind. Additionally, you can sip your warm or cold drink for a taste sensation. By the way, you might do something like this with an indoor or outdoor spa if you prefer. The environment is designed to immerse you in an experience with some of your favorite things. Recognize the inherent self-kindness of this act.

Imagine if your partner ran you a bath or turned on the spa, put rose petals in it, set up the candles, placed a glass of wine nearby, and turned on some soft music. Maybe you were blindfolded and you were escorted into the room with this surprise. You'd probably think, "Oh my God, you're so romantic. This is so kind of you to do this and you have all my favorite things. How wonderful." Yet, you don't express that gratitude to yourself when you do this act for yourself. You don't say, "Thank you for putting all these beautiful, luxurious things together to create this really warm, nurturing, and supportive environment so I can relax and let the week go."

More than likely, you've created this wonderful environment for yourself unconsciously, unintentionally. As many self-care advocates say, "Make the unconscious conscious." Enjoy the beauty of your routines and do them intentionally.

For another variation of this, let's say you schedule a massage. You're paying someone else to give you that massage. It's still an act of self-kindness to take care of yourself. A voice in your head might say, "Ooh, I'm getting away with something. I'm going to get a massage." Or, you say, "I'm damn well going to get a massage because I earned it." But instead, you can say, "I've created this time in this environment to be kind to myself, good to myself. I want to nurture and take care of myself."

It may be a matter of just fixing your favorite meal, reading a book that makes you laugh, or watching a show that can take you away to another time or place. Maybe you decide to meditate, make time for a hobby, participate in a recreational activity, or just do something that's fun and brings you joy.

You'll find that as you do these random acts of self-kindness for yourself, they carry you away to another place. Think of it as a space where you can completely release your grip on your day, your week, your reality.

All of these acts of self-kindness should be done intentionally. It's when you make the unconscious conscious and you're acknowledging that it's been a challenging week, or even a couple of hours. When you decide to do this thing for yourself, you're creating this space.

In your conscious mind, you may tell yourself you're escaping. Invariably, what happens is that what you're doing isn't enjoyable because of this attitude. Perhaps it's enjoyable in the moment. Then when you stop doing what you're doing, you begin to beat yourself up. You think of all the things that you could have been doing instead of that relaxing or enjoyable activity.

Know that you can flip the script. You can do these things for yourself intentionally to take care of yourself. For instance, you might watch a movie instead of doing a work assignment because the assignment is stressing you out or you've hit a roadblock. Embrace taking time to give yourself some space to intentionally and fully enjoy an activity. Recognize that you've hit a wall or need to step away for a bit, by saying "I'm going to give myself some time to recalibrate, recharge, and come back to the work with a different perspective."

In my case, I might take a walk. Perhaps I'll fix something to eat or drink. I might stop for the whole day and not pick up that other activity until the next day. It doesn't matter what the situation is. What matters is that my wisdom and discernment told me that it's time to take a step back. By discernment, I mean our better judgement or gut feeling. And I've listened to that. I've understood my own signals that it's time to take a break from something. Then, I've curated an event, activity, or environment to care for myself during my letting-go phase.

When you take a step back, try to do something completely different so you can return to the task with a fresh perspective. This doesn't turn the activity you did into an escape from a problem or a bad decision. It's a way to adjust your mental state. Also, it's a way to move your body, your emotions, and your mind to create a different landscape. Importantly, this is a different way of seeing a situation which can be very productive on many levels.

The issue with welcoming these intentional acts typically arises when you start the self-beating cycle, thinking in terms of wasting time instead of doing what you need to do. Often that's even though your wisdom and your discernment told you that it was time to stop a troublesome activity for a little while. Sometimes you might listen to the wisdom, but you beat yourself up for it anyway. Remember that listening to your wisdom is only step one and step two is doing something that allows you the space for a different perspective. It doesn't matter what that thing is but do it consciously and intentionally.

Chapter 19
Thoughts About Faith and Intuition

As human beings, we each adopt different interpretations of faith and intuition. These are different influences that move us in different directions. My faith has always been based on a belief in a higher power. I've called it God, yet I have no religious association with the word God because I wasn't a religious child and I'm not a religious adult. But my entire life, that higher power to me has been God. So that's what I call faith.

My faith and intuition are tied together. I do understand how many people deal with them separately. Perhaps the best way to explain this is in a story.

I was about eight years old and we were living in Arizona. My family—meaning my stepfather, mother, brother, and sister—spent the day with another family, my aunt, my uncle, and my cousins. We were out in dry, sandy wash-beds. These are areas that accumulate water during monsoon season to reduce flooding downstream. We were four-wheeling when one of the trucks became stuck, all the way up to the axles. We stopped and everyone started looking for objects they could place around the tires to gain some traction.

In that moment, I had a very unusual experience. It was as if I was moving backwards away from where everyone was frantically trying to get the vehicle unstuck. Similar to other chaotic situations that happened in our lives, my family became angry, violent and they immediately concluded that it had to be someone's fault. They shouted at each other and called each other names. It was incredibly tense, and the incident quickly turned very dark.

When something like this happens to "normal" people, they often laugh about it and the situation can turn into a comedy of errors. Yet for me in that moment, I was once again surrounded by the craziness that was my family and extended family. Stress always equaled violence and darkness.

As I started to feel like I was being pulled away from the scene taking place across the bank of the wash-bed, I suddenly had a feeling of complete safety envelope me. It was a sense of warmth and safety with a kind of male energy. Then I heard and felt a voice say, "You're going to be safe. You're going to be fine." It was clear to me that this reassurance was a message from a place of faith but also deep intuition to "get ready to weather a storm and know you'll be okay."

I remember my whole body responding to that "voice" in a way that helped me understand it was true. For me, my faith and intuition were tied together in a comforting and lasting way during and after that event. Some people would call it a feeling in their gut, while others might have another somatic, or bodily, type of experience. Something resonated inside me, as it could within all of us at times.

After this experience, perhaps because I was so young, I've considered that energetic resonance inextricably tied to both my intuition and my faith. Meaning, if there is an energetic resonance when I take the time to consider a decision, then I consider that my inner confirmation from both my faith and my intuition.

I've learned over time to pay attention to those feelings, as they reflect wisdom for me. A case with me not respecting my intuition occurred a couple of years before Sam passed when I was looking for an independent groomer. I really disliked leaving Charlie and Sam in a salon, where they'd be in cages and stressed out. When I went to the salon I immediately felt a knot in my stomach. I didn't feel right, but because I'd been told so many times how paranoid I was that I just ignored my feelings. I assumed I was being silly and left my dogs.

It turned out that I felt sick to my stomach the whole time they were there. I was nervously pacing waiting for the groomer to call to say my dogs were ready to pick up. Later that evening we ended up at the emergency veterinarian because the groomer had injured Sam. I was so angry with myself for not listening to those feelings. I should have apologized and left, but I abandoned myself and poor Sam paid the price. It wasn't a significant injury, but it would have been avoided had I trusted my intuition.

Call it faith in myself, faith in a higher power, or call it intuition, but I find when I listen to those messages I avoid most unpleasant situations. To me these influences are one in the same. This makes me wonder if you've had experiences like mine in which you acted on a "feeling" for a good outcome or failed to do so and the results were not good. How strongly do you believe in your intuition and faith when making decisions?

Chapter 20
Make Change Normal

The people in our lives are accustomed to us being a certain way. This means the way we talk, present ourselves, approach life, dress, and behave in various situations. Our family, close friends, extended relatives, colleagues, peers, and any groups we're affiliated with in the community believe that they know who we are by these characteristics.

Few of those people are privy to or have any idea about the more traumatic experiences we've endured in our lives. That's because we create boundaries and curate the persona—the self—who shows up when around them. It's like the *self* who's around family is different from the *self* at work. Those may be different from the one who shows up with friends for a happy hour.

There are different nuances to who we are and how we show up around different people.

We all have masks we wear in life as we hit a transformational moment and start taking steps to move away from our past. It's when we start to read books and maybe engage with therapy of some type. This is the point when we start to make some big changes in our life.

Maybe you begin to enforce more boundaries. Perhaps you start a new job or quit your job to start doing something different. It could be that you leave a partner or spouse. Maybe you terminate or re-establish relationships with members of your family. All these actions are possible as you shift and change.

One thing you must understand is that the people around you may or may not shift and change with you or accept the changes you're making. After all, there are some people who rely upon you the way you are. If you change certain characteristics, that will disrupt those relationships.

I don't say this to discourage you from embarking on your path nor to disparage anyone in your life. I say this to alert you about the perceptions and expectations embedded in these relationships. If you know you're in a toxic relationship and you're seeking a way to get out of it, there will be strife in your exiting it. There also are other relationships that might be affected by your changes in less obvious ways. Some individuals may rely on you to be in your current frame of mind because it's similar to theirs.

Like attracts like. If you're wondering why you're constantly feeling negative or drained, look at who you spend your time with, what music you listen to, what television shows you watch, what video games you play. You get the idea, just look at your environment.

I should add that there may be people in the constellation of your life who rely on you being melancholy, quiet, or always a bit down. They may not see you as being in crisis necessarily, just not happy. Think of Eeyore in the *Winnie the Pooh* tales. They need you to feed them a type of energy from your melancholy. If you read a couple of books, start seeing a coach or therapist, and begin to change, those individuals may not be happy for you. They may not praise or congratulate you for your progression to Tigger (another *Winnie the Pooh* character) style energy.

People in your life who aren't doing some type of introspective work may even be resentful when you begin to change your way of being and the way you connect with them. This can be quite challenging, particularly if what you're dealing with is belonging, self-esteem, or abandonment issues. Having people move away from you because you're becoming happier or more peaceful can be quite traumatizing. You could feel like you're doing something wrong, again.

I thought I was doing a good thing for myself and others close to me by trying to be better. But I found I was losing friends. To that, I just want to say I'm sorry that's the experience you may have, but it definitely can be part of the experience. My relationships prior to my healing journey could not be described as real friendships. Those friends were there when they needed me the most, not vice versa. Part of this was because I never said no. Why would I? I didn't have any family. All I had was friends and colleagues. I figured I'd do whatever they wanted me to do because I needed people in my life.

When I began to build more strength and have more self-respect, I started to establish boundaries. I learned that saying no is a complete sentence that doesn't require further explanation. This resulted in some people falling away from my life and it was remarkably hurtful. I cried, even sobbed over people who left my life who weren't good for me. Their influence and their energies weren't good for me. They never really cared about me, only about a version of me. Yet it was challenging for me to let go, especially as one who was seeking community and belonging. It sounds odd, but I actually needed to remove people from my life to have a life.

I needed to be part of a community of people with whom I felt safe and comfortable. These would be people with whom I could be my authentic self. Sometimes being your authentic self can be messy, but that's part of the journey. Just know that people stepping away from you as you create a better environment for yourself is a natural part of the process. Don't doubt or question yourself. Don't beat yourself up about it either. What you need to do is be your own best friend. On those long rainy nights, it's much more comforting, nurturing, and soothing to have the right people around you rather than those who contort you into someone that you're not.

Understand that this is part of your journey. Parts will be painful, but not all. You'll learn something and you'll be much better as you avoid those harmful situations. Sometimes you'll take two steps forward and maybe ten steps back. It's natural and it happens to everyone as part of the process.

Realize that you'll encounter tough days, when you hope your phone rings or you wish you had someone to talk to, but all you have is yourself. Yet, those can be the most rewarding times. They're the moments when you come home to yourself. It's when you learn who you are and what you're made of on the inside. As lonely and isolating as that can feel in the moment, there will be a time when that self-knowledge is thrilling and exciting. It'll be an opening, not a closing. Keep that in mind.

Understand that not all the shifts and changes will feel positive and uplifting. But all the feelings, the loss, the separation, and coming to know yourself will be incredibly important and necessary in your sacred journey.

Chapter 21
The Sacred Journey

It's been ten years since my red light moment. That was the moment I knew everything in my life needed to change. I can say confidently and honestly that I'm a completely different person today than I was back then. I did, in fact, change every single aspect of my life.

The one constant from my red light moment to today has been my dog, Charlie. I credit him as one of my primary motivators for getting me through all the challenges and changes over those ten years. There has always been a walk, a pet, a cuddle, and a game of fetch. Charlie has been such a blessing. It's astonishing what unconditional love can do for a person, even when that love is being given by an animal. No matter what kind of day I've had, Charlie has been ecstatic to see me the moment I walked through my door. His love has been a game-changer for me.

I've learned that we all need a pet, person, anthem, activity, song, or other "rock" in our lives as a positive influence. They can transport us to a place where we know we're okay. It's natural for them to change over time, but it's important to have an influence like that especially during the challenging times in our journey.

Charlie has seen me become a completely different person. I still have the same memories and past. However, I live with that in relative peace and in a type of partnership with them. All the experiences, even the truly hard ones, were necessary for me to become who I am now. I have no regrets about anything. Period. That's because I think it's a waste of energy to feel regret. This is especially the case because the lessons I learned and the wisdom I gained from the extremely hard times serve me well today. Regrets would diminish a portion of who I am now. And I won't do that.

I won't say that I don't have bad days, moments of depression or insecurity. All that hasn't magically disappeared. But my relationship with all of it has changed. My relationship with myself has changed. I now live with all this in the ecosystem that's my life. And I allow for the wisdom from the past to help me as I chart my path forward.

My point with all this is that we can each benefit from the wisdom that comes from many types of experiences along our journeys. Those in our lives contribute greatly to the quality of our lives. They can help us get through the rough days and dark periods, because we know that life journeys aren't linear. I can't help but think of Charlie on walks and playing. His path is always here and there due to new sights, smells, sounds, and just plain curiosity. He lives in the moment, soaking up experiences. It comes naturally to him and obviously brings him joy.

This same type of boundless curiosity opens up once you begin your sacred journey. It's how you find yourself, your heart, your center, your hope, and your sense of peace. Your task is to contextualize your journey to take you where you want to go.

For me, this journey of healing was away from all the abuse, violence, and patterns that had shaped my family. I wanted more peace, happiness, playfulness, joy, and community. That was my journey. Your journey will focus on whatever change is necessary to create the life you want to live.

Along my journey of healing, I've gained an entirely different level of compassion. It's not just for other people due to the things they've endured and experiences they've had. It's compassion for myself for finally coming to understand that I'm not a pariah.

I now recognize that my childhood was so isolating it was impossible to share or talk about my stories, let alone discuss them with anyone who had anything in common with me. It was my own world I had created within myself for my own survival. And it was inconceivable that other people lived like that, too.

Because it can be extremely challenging to seek help in an isolationist environment, I feel incredibly lucky to have encountered the people who created wonderful, sacred opportunities for me to grow and heal. Those who gave me the chance to continue becoming who I wanted to be, the person I continue to strive to become.

I hope that having heard part of my story inspires you to begin to process your own experiences. Maybe it can help you to feel like you're not alone in pursuing your path. I understand that it can be uncomfortable to think about, let alone share these intimate feelings and issues. It's still complicated for me. It's a deeply private and personal decision to share with even the most trusted professionals, friends, and family members.

Maybe what I can do is encourage you to first seek counsel with your inner authority. Trust your intuition to determine what's right for you. It's okay if you feel this must be a secret from everyone in your life. If that secret is improving your health, your state of mind, your place in the world, then you must do what's best for you. There's absolutely no one else who can live your life for you. Your pain and your suffering are personal to you. But so is your happiness, peace, and joy.

Whatever choices you make in your life to reduce your suffering and pain while increasing your joy, peace, and happiness are your personal decisions. And they must be between you and your inner authority, your inner knowing. That's because they'll become the tapestry of the experiences in your new world.

I would say the most important point behind everything I've said and will continue to say is to be your own advocate, your own best friend, your own empowering force, and your own hero. The level of self-compassion and healing you can achieve in that space will determine the level of your peace. It will bring about your happiness and joy. It'll even enhance your connectivity to those around you. Whatever decisions you make and whatever tools and methods you use, I encourage you to stand by them with all the power that you hold as an individual and keep putting one foot in front of the other.

I do want to emphasize that this journey never ends. There's no finish line to cross where everything's perfect after that. I believe the journey ends when we take our last breath. Prior to that, I think the unfolding of your journey leads you to who you're going to be. As long as you allow life to affect you, to move you and your heart, your journey evolves. It morphs and it changes direction. Your purpose changes, too. It grows and develops as a result of your experiences.

I've found that no one book, class, coach, advisor, or seminar holds the keys to the kingdom of ideal change. Instead, we experience an ever-unfolding journey that's a process of discovering who we are and what we want our world to become. So much is defined by how we move forward, both separately and together. It's vital to understand that each of us has our own story to live.

I can say after ten years on my journey that the peace, joy, and happiness that's part of my life today is simply remarkable. In fact, it's indescribable in a positive way. Based on where I began and knowing where I am today, I can only imagine that I'll continue to experience more joy, peace, happiness, and playfulness even with life's ups and downs. And Charlie continues to bounce and wag his tail when I come home. He is a warrior!

I invite you to take a first step into your journey. Whatever that journey is, whatever the outcome is that you're looking for. It's worth it because it's for you. No one else can embark on your unique journey. And may your forever unfold in a way that makes you feel happy and joyful and playful and peaceful and loved. Stay curious.

Rebel

The Rebel is really an emperor because he has broken the chains of society's repressive conditioning and opinions. His very way of being is rebellious — not because he is fighting against anybody or anything, but because he has discovered his own true nature and is determined to live in accordance with it.

Commentary based on description by Deva Padma.
OSHO Zen Tarot.

Rebel Resources

Why do I keep using the term *rebel?* First, because it was a nickname from my family, which was never meant to be a compliment. So of course, I've found a way to make it one! Also, I came across this definition which to me embodies the very essence of personal empowerment and radical individuality. This is my encouragement to us all!

Many of the tools I've employed have been outside the norm, which also is fairly rebellious! I've included a list of some of the resources from my journey. However, we're all different with different experiences, so these resources may or may not resonate with you. Also, I'm not suggesting that you use the same tools I have. I'm just hoping to show you, through my own travels, the array of methods and resources available in the ethos that is the self-help world. Anything that sparks your curiosity is worth investigating further.

One personal example I'll mention here is Kundalini Yoga, specifically as taught through The Life Force Academy (LFA) by founder Jai Dev Singh. For years, I resisted and even berated the idea of meditation. I'm an extrovert so the very idea of sitting quietly felt like an antithesis to by very being. It's my nature to be in nearly constant movement, even when I'm "relaxing" at home. I stumbled onto LFA on social media. Jai Dev was leading a guided meditation and I was curious, so I attended. In the session prior to the meditation, Jai Dev led us through some intense body and breathing exercises. A bonus was that the music was sensational! You might find it hard to believe but I was actually tired from meditation. My husband and I have been active participants with LFA for two years and it's been remarkable. Had I not allowed myself to be curious, I would have passed on this type of meditation. That would have been shame.

On your self-discovery journey, do your best to remain curious and the whole world will open up.

Books

A Radical Approach to the Akashic Records, Master Your Life and Raise Your Vibration, by Melissa Feick

Advanced ThetaHealing Harnessing the Power of All That Is, by Vianna Stibal

Archetypes, A beginner's Guide to You Inner-Net, by Caroline Myss

Awaken the Giant Within, How to Take Immediate Control of Your Mental, Emotional, Physical and Financial Destiny!, by Tony Robbins

Braving the Wilderness, The Quest for True Belonging and the Courage to Stand Alone, by Brene Brown

Breaking the Habit of Being Yourself, by Dr. Joe Dispenza

Dare to Lead, Brave Work. Tough Conversations. Whole Hearts., by Brene Brown

Daring Greatly, How the Courage to be Vulnerable Transforms the Way We Live, Love, Parent, and Lead, by Brene Brown

Don't Suffer, Communicate!, by Cheri Huber and Ashwini Narayanan

Empathipedia, Healing for Empaths and Highly Sensitive Persons, by Dave Markowitz

Hold me Tight, Seven Conversations for a Lifetime of Love, by Dr. Sue Johnson

I Don't Want to, I Don't Feel Like it, How Resistance Controls Your Life and What To Do About It, by Cheri Huber and Ashwini Narayanan

Keys to the Enneagram, by A.H. Almaas

Practicing the Power of Now, by Eckhart Tolle

Resilient, How to Grow An Unshakable Core of Calm, Strength, and Happiness, by Rick Hanson

Rising Strong, How the Ability to Reset, Transforms the Way We Live, Love, Parent, and Lead, by Brene Brown

Sacred Contracts, Awakening Your Divine Potential, by Caroline Myss

Self-Compassion, The Proven Power of Being Kind to Yourself, by Kristin Neff

Seven Planes of Existence, The Philosophy of the ThetaHealing Technique, by Vianna Stibal

Sins of the Family, Becoming the Redemptive Generation, by Beverly Hubble Tauke

Taming Your Gremlin, A Surprisingly Simple Method for Getting Out of Your Own Way, by Rick Carson

The Body Keeps the Score: Brain, Mind and Body in the Healing of Trauma, by Bessel Van Der Kolk

The Enneagram of Passions and Virtues, Finding the Way Home, by Sandra, Maitri

The Gifts of Imperfection, Let Go of Who You Think You're Supposed to Be and Embrace Who You Are, by Brene Brown

The Psychedelic Explorer's Guide, Safe, Therapeutic and Sacred Journeys, by James Fadiman

The Spiritual Dimension if the Enneagram, Nine Faces of the Soul, by Sandra Maitri

The Untethered Soul, The Journey Beyond Yourself, by Michael A. Singer

There Is Nothing Wrong With You, Going Beyond Self-Hate, by Cheri Huber

ThetaHealing: You and the Creator: Deepen Your Connection with the Energy of Creation, by Vianna Stibal

Untamed, by Glennon Doyle

What You Practice is What You Have, A Guide to Having the Life You Want, by Cheri Huber

YouTube Videos

I've watched hundreds of YouTube videos on trauma, PTSD, C-PTSD, healing from abuse, spiritual awakening, energy healing, plant medicine, and so on. YouTube is a fantastic research tool to find people, organizations, and potential helpful modalities to assist in your journey.

Organizations

Tara Brach, tarabrach.com
Tara Brach is known across the world for her speaking and meditation practices. Her website has hundreds of different types of meditations, along with hundreds of talks she has given throughout her storied career. Specifically, there are several of her meditations that do not have a bell at the end. These mediations have been game-changers to enable falling asleep. Tara is a fantastic spiritual teacher.

Life Force Academy, jaidevsingh.com
Jai Dev Singh is the founder of Life Force Academy (LFA). This organization has a variety of courses and practices. They facilitate multiple immersions each year. The practices move your body, mind, and spirit toward a place of equilibrium with the ever-changing energy of life. Jai Dev's teachings are engaging, and he has an excellent sense of humor, which I appreciate. Much of the music used is performed by The Simrit Band, including Jai Dev's wife. The music itself will move you to another dimension. This is a fabulous organization to help get in touch with a more active meditation style.

Multidisciplinary Association for Psychedelic Studies (MAPS), maps.org
MAPS is a research facility in California working with psychedelics to document how they are helping in human studies on PTSD, trauma, and other debilitating disorders. This is a great

institution to follow to understand where the research is and what results they are seeing through their trials. It was helpful for me to understand more broadly how psychedelics are being studied and used to help people recover from a variety of conditions.

Zen Monastery Peace Center, Living Compassion, visitmurphys.com and livingcompassion.org
This organization has since relocated to Washington State. Cheri Huber still runs it. They have excellent programs and retreats.

Made in the USA
Middletown, DE
23 February 2023